MICHIGAN MEMORIES

INSIDE BO SCHEMBECHLER'S FOOTBALL SCRAPBOOK

by Bo Schembechler with Dan Ewald

Library of Congress Cataloging-in-Publication Data:

Schembechler, Bo.
Michigan memories: inside Bo Schembechler's football scrapbook/Bo
Schembechler with Dan Ewald.
p.   cm.
ISBN 1-886947-44-9
1. Schembechler, Bo   2. Football coaches–United States-Biography.   3.
Michigan Wolverines (Football team)–History.   4. University of Michigan–
Football–History. I. Ewald, Dan.   II. Title.
GV939.S33A3   1998
796.332'092–dc21   98-34925
[B]   CIP

Sleeping Bear Press
121 South Main Street
P.O. Box 20
Chelsea, MI 48118
www.sleepingbearpress.com

Printed and bound in the United States.

10 9 8 7 6 5 4 3 2 1

Inquiries regarding prints of Joseph Arcure's photographs contained in this
book should be made at 800/761-3686 ext. 50 or at www.foto1.com.

The essence of Michigan Football lies not in the bodies of all those magnificent players who bravely take the field each Saturday in the fall. It lives proudly, rather, in the spirit of all the players, all the coaches, all the students, all the alumni and all the fans.

For all the men and women — past, present and future — who strive for excellence through honesty, integrity and hard work, this book belongs to you. That's the Michigan way.

— Bo Schembechler

ACKNOWLEDGMENTS

The authors wish to acknowledge all of the former University of Michigan Football players, coaches and staff who contributed so generously and unselfishly to the creation of this book. In addition, a special thanks is extended to Howard Wikel, Greg Kinney, Lloyd Carr, Don Lund, Don Dufek, Cathy Schembechler, Lynne Johnson, the Bentley Historical Library and the University of Michigan Sports Media Relations Department.

FOREWORD

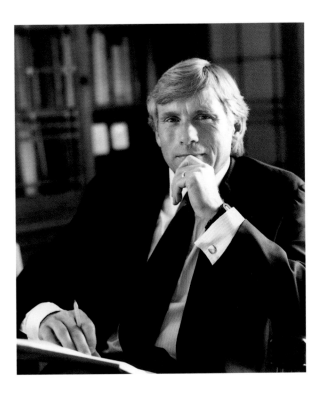

When I was Dean of the University of Michigan Law School, we invited the former President of Yale University, Bart Giamatti, to deliver the Cook Lectures, a prestigious lecture series sponsored every year on a subject related to "American institutions." Although President Giamatti was a scholar of Renaissance literature, he also was an avid sports fan; and, in fact, had recently become the commissioner of baseball. Highly intelligent, cultured, and eloquent, Giamatti had been invited to the University to speak on the matter of sport in American life. We needed, according to custom, someone to introduce Giamatti, and I chose Bo Schembechler.

The three of us gathered in my office before the lecture. By background or profession, these two men shared little in common, yet they were drawn to each other by the force of the other's personality. What they shared was charisma, and their conversation revelled in that common bond. In his essay, "Character," Ralph Waldo Emerson reflected on the peculiar fact that the reputations of many great figures in history cannot be explained or accounted for by their actual deeds or words. To Emerson something "resided in these men which begot an expectation that outran all their performance. The largest part of their power was latent." This Emerson calls "Character—a reserved force which acts directly by presence and without means." Without wishing to overpraise Bo, and thereby discredit what I have to say about him, I believe that it is precisely this quality of character—of a latent power—that is the single most important fact we all sense in him.

Over the years I have, of course, run into many of Bo's former players. The conversation is always the same. It begins with a discussion of what an incredible coach Bo was, and then invariably the subject becomes what an extraordinary person Bo is. As with so many individuals possessing a magnetic personality, Bo seems to have been a never-ending fountain of humorous actions. Everyone has a Bo story, or several. But they are always told with a touch of awe and love for the man.

I cannot speak authoritatively about what Bo accomplished as a football coach. It seems to me truly exceptional, and pretty much everyone else thinks similarly. But I can say that he is one of those few individuals around whom an institution, whether it is a team or a university, takes shape and substance. And for this reason, it will always be a source of the deepest pride for us that Bo Schembechler was part of the making of the University of Michigan.

—Lee C. Bollinger

TABLE OF CONTENTS

INTRODUCTION

Bo Schembechler likes to think of himself as nothing more than "the ol' football coach." He didn't create the Michigan Football tradition. Fielding H. Yost beat him by about seven decades on that one.

Bo wasn't a football revolutionary. Fritz Crisler handled that with his inception of the two-platoon system and the famous winged helmets. Bo's preference was to "hit 'em clean." But also "hit 'em hard and often."

Bo's contribution to Michigan tradition touches another level. He's the godfather of the contemporary Michigan program. As former Athletic Director Don Canham simply states, "None of this would have happened if it hadn't been for Bo."

What Canham refers to is the most celebrated, successful, and revered college football tradition in the country.

Of course, Bo scoffs at the suggestion of his importance. That's exactly what "the ol' football coach" would do.

The numbers are staggering:

- More wins — 194 — than any coach in Michigan history.
- 13 Big Ten championships in a 21-year tenure.
- 17 post-season bowl games, including 10 Rose Bowls.
- 17 top-ten finishes in the final wire service polls.

As overwhelming as the numbers are, that's all they are — numbers. Bo is proud of them. But his strength is leading people and the spirit that he breathed into the proud Michigan tradition.

"Obviously he knows football," said former Michigan All-American Dan Dierdorf. "But he knows people even better. Bo has the ability to get a whole organization driving in the same direction. Not just the players, but all the coaches and assistants and secretaries and everyone that goes into making a successful organization."

Bo came to Michigan in 1969 when the program needed a little boost, at a time when college football was beginning to explode across national television networks.

The game was becoming big...very big. With Canham's genius for marketing and Bo's relentless drive for excellence, Michigan Football was propelled to the top of intercollegiate sports.

Now the game has grown into an industry of its own. Interest across the country borders on religious zeal. Revenues generated from those Saturday afternoons boggle the mind.

While the evolution is impressive, it's also extracted its price. The magnitude of the college football universe may have marked the end to such romantically colorful single-name figures such as Bo and Woody and The Bear.

Certainly the intensity of the Michigan-Ohio State rivalry increases each year. But what true Michigan fan doesn't miss that special tingle of the war within a war when Bo took on Woody and all those nasty boys from down south of the Michigan border?

For Bo, everything was simple. There was no hidden agenda. His focus was simple — make Michigan Men out of the boys he brought to the University and make the University proud of winning the right way.

Everything was done according to his three simple unbending principles of honesty, integrity, and hard work.

Bo was confident that his system would work. He also recognized the unique combination of academic and athletic excellence which only Michigan enjoys.

"That's the beauty about Bo," said Jim Brandstatter, one of his former players and a current radio and television analyst. "He never compromises his principles. I could see why a mother and father would feel good about sending their son to play for Bo and get an education at Michigan."

While Bo now is content that the program is in excellent hands under Coach Lloyd Carr and Athletic Director Tom Goss, he should also take pride that the program is on course precisely because of his relentless pursuit of excellence.

No one coach or player or administrator is bigger than the program as a whole. As Bo himself always preached, "It's the team...the team...the team!"

Neither Bo nor anyone else would suggest that the Michigan Football tradition would have failed to thrive without him.

But his magnificent presence for those 21 very special years is still felt today.

In the following pages, "the ol' football coach" has assembled a scrapbook of Michigan memories. Many are personal ones that he had a hand in shaping. Others reflect the history of this staggering tradition.

Bo learned from this long tradition and then contributed chapters of his own before carefully passing on the program in excellent shape.

He now shares some memories that mean so much to so many people. There are glimpses of various personalities. There are pictures and stories of events that help to shape this singular tradition.

And there is assurance that this marvelous history will continue to be written in the Michigan way.

—Dan Ewald

THAT'S TRADITION!

Tradition is something you can't bottle. You can't buy it at the corner store. But it is there to sustain you when you need it most. I've called upon it time and time again. And so have countless other Michigan athletes and coaches. There is nothing like it. I hope it never dies.

— Fritz Crisler

t's been more than a half-century since Fritz Crisler defined the University of Michigan tradition. It's as alive today as it was back then. And it will still be alive a hundred years from now.

Here's exactly what Fritz was saying.

Tra-DI-tion is having one of the finest academic institutions in the country.

Tra-DI-tion is a football program that has put together more victories than any Division I school in history.

Tra-DI-tion is running that program with integrity and according to all the rules.

Tra-DI-tion is more than 105,000 people in a stadium almost 75-years-old every football Saturday.

Tra-DI-tion is all the color and tailgating and spirit that comes together to make all those Saturdays in Ann Arbor like no other place in the whole United States of America.

That's Michigan Football.

THAT'S *tra-DI-tion!*

Tradition is a feeling. That's what it really is. It's a feeling that links the past to the present and builds a bridge to the future.

A lot of schools talk about tradition. But there is nothing like the tradition that lives at the University of Michigan.

We have it in our academic program. We have it throughout our campus.

And as sure as there are no greater helmets than those famous Michigan winged ones anywhere in the world, we have it in our football program.

First of all, when you talk about the University of Michigan, you're talking about as great a public

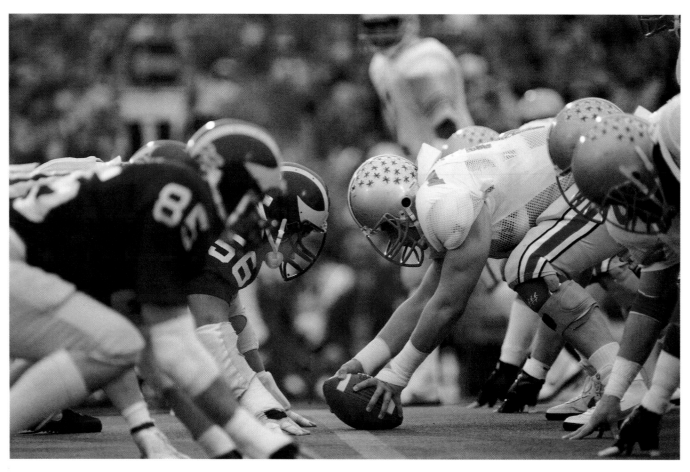

"Tra-DI-tion breeds in-TEN-si-ty."

institution as there is in America. It has attracted the brightest young people from all over the country and, nowadays, from all over the world.

Once all those people come to the university, they discover that part of that great tradition is Michigan Football.

It's those 105,000 people in that old red brick stadium. It's the great rivalries of Michigan and Ohio State...Michigan and Notre Dame...Michigan and Michigan State. It's reaching back to make one more great play when there's nothing left to give but determination alone.

THAT'S tradition!

After those young students graduate and move on to pursue careers all over the world, Michigan Football remains as a link to their university. During the whole week of every football season, they can hear about their team playing back at Michigan. And they know exactly what to expect.

They expect excellence. They expect winning according to all the rules. They can picture in their minds that whole spectacle going on back in Ann Arbor. It's their connection to the past.

The Michigan Football program must remain one of the finest in the country. With nationally ranked schools such as law and business and engineering and medicine and all the others, tradition challenges the Michigan Football program. It MUST always remain among the national elite.

We have built a football program here that will last. Anyone who has participated in it knows why it's so great. Anyone who has become attached to the program as a supporter or a fan shares in that tremendous pride. Michigan Football was built within the rules and it lives within the rules.

I don't believe you can have the tradition of Michigan Football without a long period of success. You don't build tradition on losing teams. No school in America has enjoyed the success of Michigan.

No other school can because no other school has won as many games as Michigan.

Tradition demands that we pass the torch from one generation to the next. For the coaches it's gone from Yost to Crisler to Schembechler to Carr. For the players it's gone from Heston to Oosterbaan to Harmon to Kramer to Dierdorf to Carter to Howard to Woodson.

Every coach, every player, every athletic director, every equipment manager, every trainer, every secretary that has worked in the football program shares in that tradition.

And so does every student, every former student and every fan who believes in a program that is more than a century old and still operates on the same principles of doing things the right way — with honesty and integrity!

Each game — from Fielding Yost's "point-a-minute" teams to the ones that are played on television screens across the nation each Saturday now — is a piece of that tradition that we call Michigan Football.

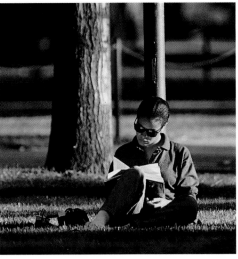

"They made it to the 1902 Rose Bowl, but today we'd NEVER take a picture with guys laying on the ground."

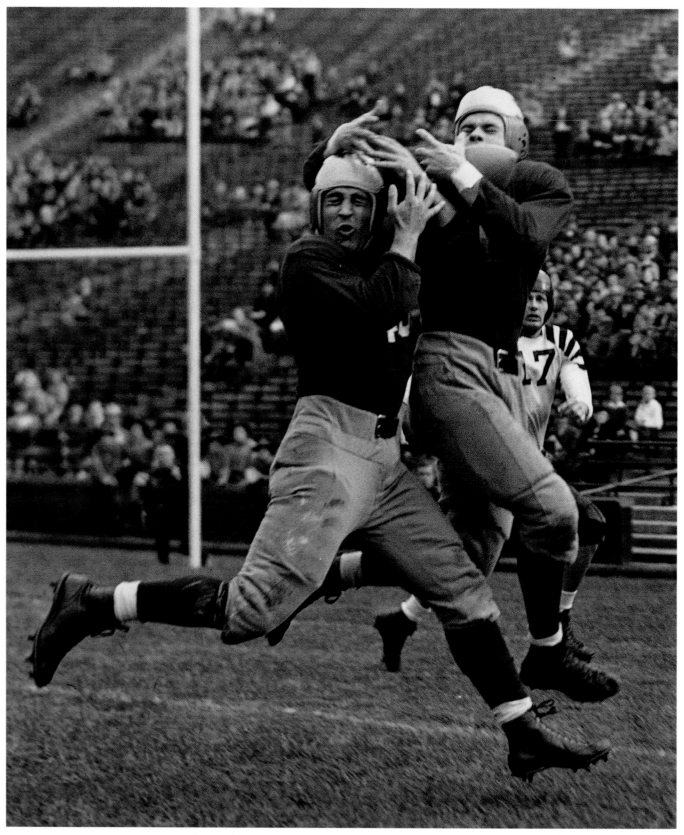

"They'd probably have their eyes open if they had worn face masks back then. Look at those empty seats. You won't see that at Michigan anymore."

All the touchdowns...all the interceptions...all the victories in the record books continually add to that tradition. Games that were won five, 10, 20, or more than 50 years ago still remain as alive today as the one played just last Saturday.

When you are able to relive all the plays and all the excitement of so many games from so long ago, that's the true measure of tradition. It just doesn't die.

The games will always be the heart of all those memories. But so many other elements are mixed into the magic of Michigan Football tradition.

There are the tailgate parties...the traffic jams to get to the games...all the Michigan flags...those airplanes flying over the stadium during the games...just the stadium itself.

Even today, every time I see that stadium I still can't imagine that Fielding Yost had the vision to construct such a masterpiece way back in 1927.

More people have watched college football in that stadium than any other facility in the world.

Just imagine — for every home game, year after year, more than 105,000 people cram into that park. For three hours during each game, that stadium holds more people than all but a handful of cities around the state.

"Great picture, but how would you like the seat of the guy who took it?"

9

"Now that's what I call punt coverage."

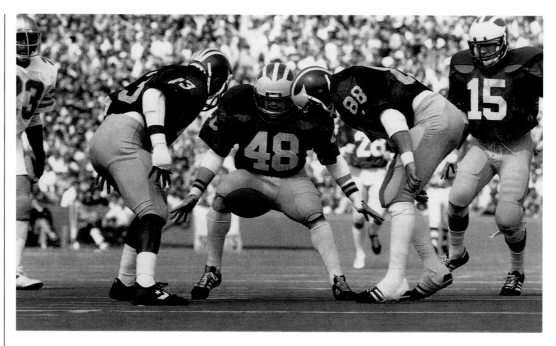

"Derrick Alexander was one of several great Michigan receivers, but he better get both hands on the ball or we're going to lose it!"

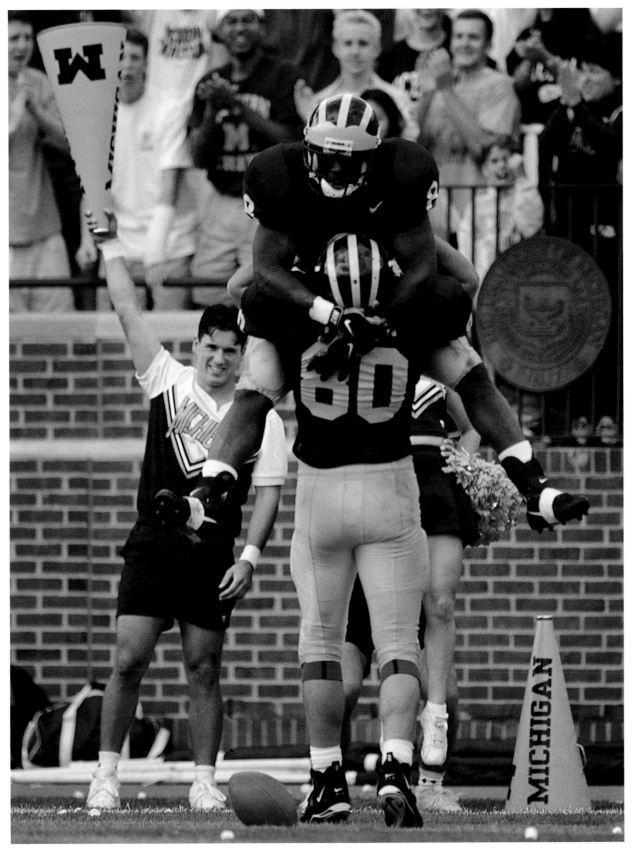

"When you tackle your own man like this, then you know there's a victory smile behind that face mask."

"When you fly over the stadium on a Michigan Football Saturday, I guess it's not a secret anymore."

"There was *never* a time running under that banner that I didn't jump up and touch it."

Each one of those people share in the Michigan Football tradition. Each one of them adds a little bit more to it.

And there isn't a bad seat in the house.

One of the most amazing parts of that stadium to me is the tunnel that leads to the field. As big as the stadium is, there's only one way onto that field. And there's only one way off.

You've got to go through that tunnel!

I'm not sure how a heavyweight champion feels when he walks up to the ring for a big fight. But it can't be any more electrifying than that walk through the tunnel to take the field for a Michigan football game.

It's dark in that tunnel when you come out of the locker room. The tunnel sort of grades down toward the field. As you get closer, it starts to get a little brighter.

Then all of a sudden, it hits you like a blinding light. When you finally line up to charge out on to that field in front of more than 105,000 screaming fans, there's absolutely no other feeling on God's earth that even comes close to matching it.

The letter winners from the other sports hold that "M" banner at the middle of the field. All of our guys jump up to touch it. That little leap is something all of our guys will cherish for the rest of their lives.

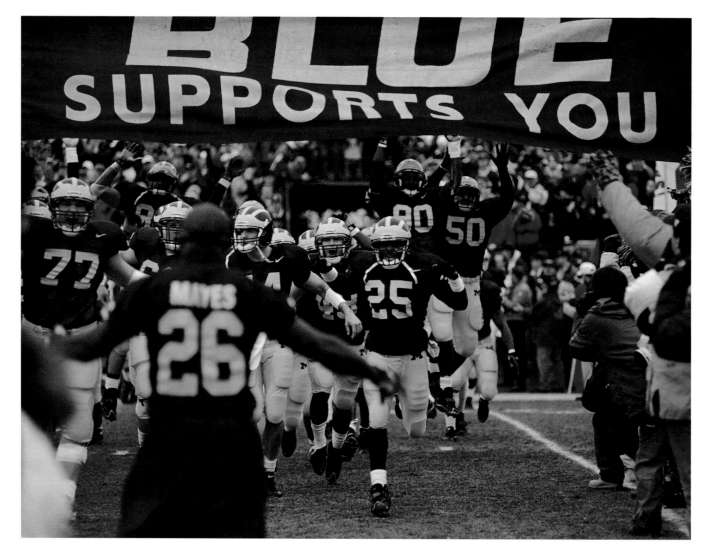

"Now do you think these guys are ready to play?"

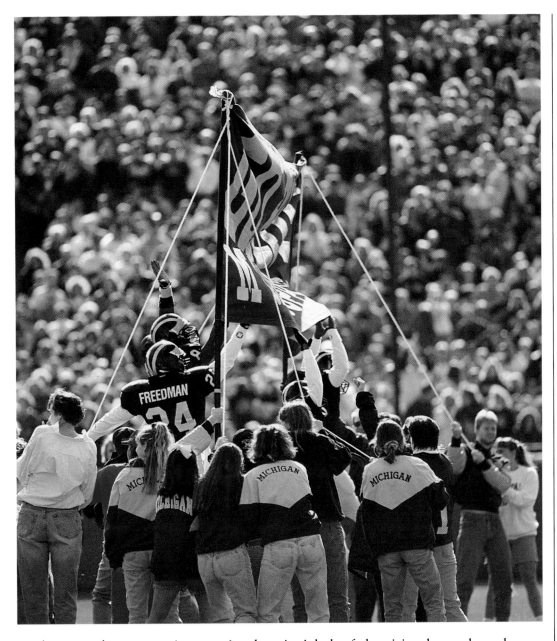

I don't care how many times you've done it. A bolt of electricity shoots through your body every time you run out of that tunnel. Even if you're just watching, goosebumps jump up all over your body.

Sitting way up in the press box, I still feel it today. I still get chills today.

There's a special feeling for the Michigan Marching Band. That band has a tradition of its very own. And it's become as much a part of Michigan tradition as the maize and blue colors themselves.

They have their own building and their own marching area. People have endowed positions in the band just as they have in football.

The band members are not all music majors. Basically, they're kids who came out of their high school bands and wanted to become part of the tradition.

Competition to make the band is just like the competition in football. It's tough. Those kids who make it, though, appreciate what they had to go through. They carry that accomplishment for life.

"I love the band. And don't for one second think it isn't part of the whole tradition."

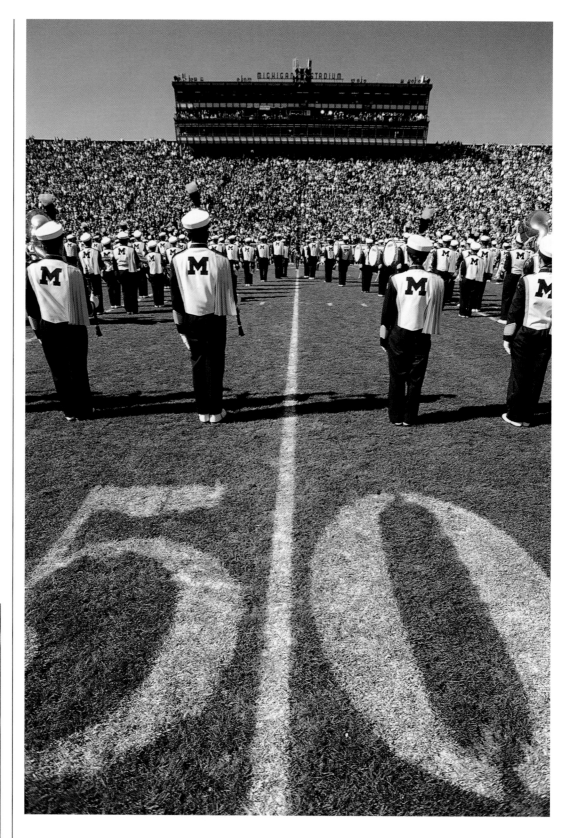

The tradition of that band goes back to Bill Revelli and George Cavender. Revelli was probably the greatest band leader of all time. People who played for him are conducting bands at other schools all over the country.

I love that band. And you better bet your boots it has an effect on the football team and all the players.

There were big games on the road when I insisted that our band go with us. We would never go to Columbus or South Bend or East Lansing without our band. I was not going to one of those schools and listen to their band without having ours there.

It was simple. We don't go without our band. That's how strongly I felt about it.

Their practice field isn't far from where the football team practices. The band would be running through their drills when we'd be running through ours.

When we were practicing for the opener or a big game, the band director would call me.

"You need me, Bo?" he'd ask.

"Yeah," I'd tell him.

"What time you want us?" he'd ask.

"Be ready at such and such a time," I'd tell him.

We'd be finishing up some drills. Then right at the time the director promised, we could hear the music as the band marched up to the practice field.

I'd call a halt to the practice. The band would surround the team and play "The Victors." All the players would sing the words. That's the greatest fight song ever written. It was a helluva scene.

THAT'S tradition!

"Look at that band. That's history from 1897."

"I had Bill Revelli come to every fall meeting of the freshmen to teach them 'The Victors' — the greatest fight song in the history of intercollegiate athletics. He was the greatest band director in Michigan history. When I got here, he was the first man to visit my office. He said, 'I run this band like you run your football team.'"

"George Cavender took over where Revelli left off."

"That's the greatest band and the greatest fans waiting to greet the Michigan team. Look how neat those people look."

At other times practicing for big games, we'd play tapes of the band. Sometimes we'd play tapes of Bob Ufer calling some key plays in a big victory from years gone by.

You can't do all these things at other schools. You can't just go out and create tradition.

It has to develop decade after decade. And it must be shaped with honesty and integrity.

All these things are part of the Michigan Football tradition. All the parties, all the music, all the banners, all the old alumni coming back to games dressed in maize and blue. Everything plays a part in the most successful college football program in history.

Tradition is the feeling someone has for the university and everything that surrounds it.

Everybody runs into tough times. Sometimes a student is having a hard time in certain classes. Sometimes the football team is trailing by a touchdown with only a few minutes left to play.

That's when you reach back and tell yourself — "Hey, man...this is Michigan. I've got to do something about that right now."

If you play here or coach here, you automatically think in terms of not letting down all those people who started that tradition years and years ago.

There's a big shadow at Michigan. What kind of shadow is there at a losing school?

It's impossible to win every game. No team can. And there are valuable lessons to learn from every loss.

At Michigan, though, it's unforgivable to walk off that field with a drop of sweat left in your body.

That's the difference.

THAT'S tradition!

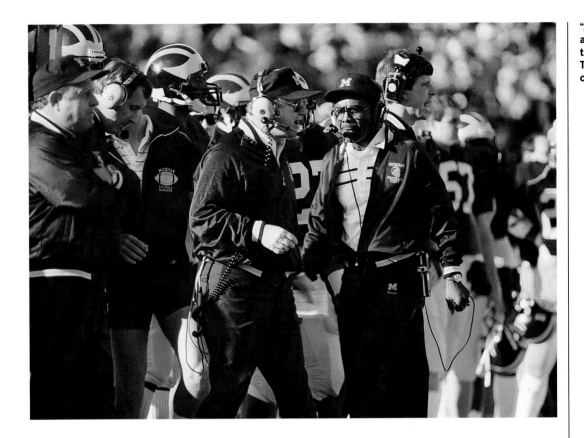

"A head coach is only as good as his assistants. I had the best. Terrell Burton was one of them."

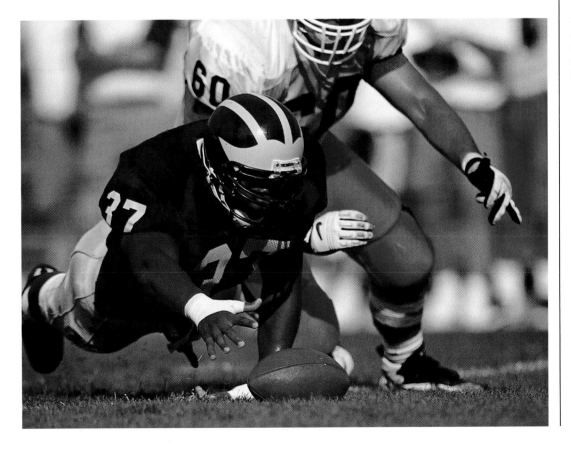

"It takes intensity and alertness to create turnovers. Then you capitalize like Jarrett Irons did."

"Inspired by an Michigan upset victory over the powerful University of Chicago, coached by the legendary Amos Alonzo Stagg, 1898, Louis Elbel created *The Victors* walking from the field. Now a century old, it remains the most celebrated college fight song in America."

"The cheerleaders get the fans ready early."

THE HOLE TO GLORY

There's a hole in Michigan Stadium that plays a game with every player's mind each Saturday even before the real game begins.

It's mid-field on the east side of the stadium. Like the ball that slowly descends each New Year's Eve in New York's Times Square, all eyes in the stadium are riveted to that hole as seconds tick down to kickoff.

It's the tunnel.

Well over 100,000 people for every game. But for players and coaches of both Michigan and their foes, there's only one way onto that magnificent field...and only one way off.

It's dark. It's dank. It's almost like some secret passageway carefully tucked away in time and used only for special — if not sacred — occasions.

It's far from aesthetically glamorous. Yet that drab concrete is richer with tradition than all the colorful murals and paintings of the world's most celebrated art galleries.

No player ever forgets his first trip down the tunnel. Even after several trips, the experience still causes shivers.

"The first time I did it I thought I was going to pee in my pants," said three-time All-American Ron Kramer. "There's no feeling like it. I can't put it into words."

As the team comes out of the locker room, players are jammed together like aspirin in a bottle. It's tight. And every person is one step from the edge.

It's shoulder pad to shoulder pad. Helmet to helmet. Every hulking player is sharing the same air. Even veteran seniors are as charged as raw freshmen.

"There is no greater feeling for player or coach than charging out of that tunnel in front of more than 100,000 people."

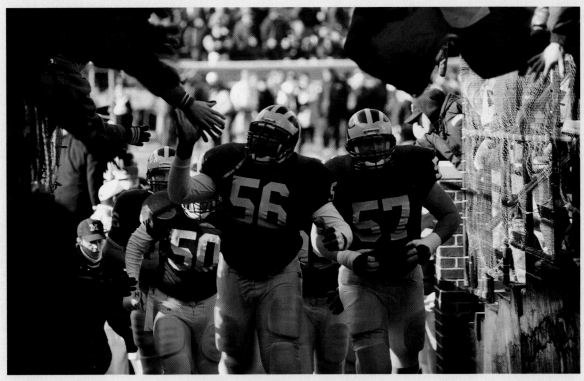

"One way in and one way out."

"When I was in school, freshmen weren't eligible," said All-American Dan Dierdorf who is a member of the National Football League Hall of Fame. "So I'd go into the stadium when it was empty and just dream about how it must feel to charge out of that tunnel.

"There's no way to describe just how big that stadium is when you come out. There's a hundred-thousand people and you can't see a single one. It's like a snapshot. One minute you're in darkness and the next you're in the middle of the whole deal. It takes your breath away."

Once that signal is made, all the players, coaches, and team personnel charge from that tunnel and leap up to touch the "M" banner which varsity athletes from other sports hold in the middle of the field.

It's emotional. It also can be intimidating.

"Some visiting coaches have a difficult time just preparing their teams to take the field here," said Terrell Burton, one of Bo's long-time assistants.

"It's mind-boggling. When you come out of that tunnel, all you see is this sea of people. Opposing teams get the feeling that not only do they have to play our team but also all these people."

For part of his career, Burton worked games from the press box.

"I'd watch how our team charged out of that tunnel," he said. "You could get a feeling of how they were going to play just by the way they took the field."

The tunnel also is a valuable recruiting tool.

"Where else in the country can you take a young man into a stadium like this and then walk him down that tunnel which creates a feeling like nothing else in the world?" Burton asks.

Nowhere. It's part of the tradition. One way in...and one way out.

SPIRIT FROM THE SIDELINES

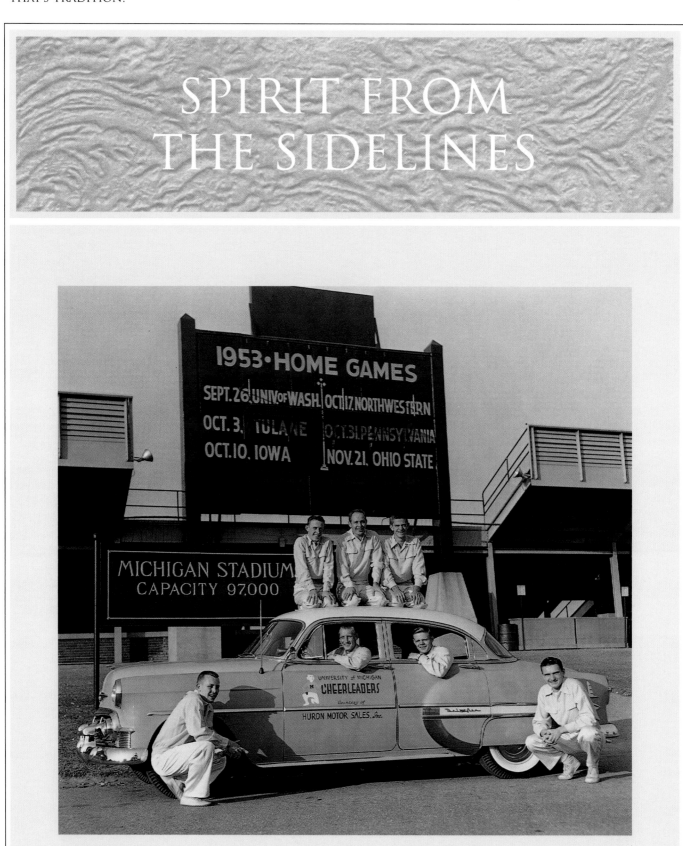

Millions of people have fallen for Michigan Football. No one, perhaps, has taken more tumbles though than Newt Loken.

The former Michigan gymnastics coach tumbled, jumped, screamed and hollered while weaving the cheerleading squad into the fabric of Michigan Football tradition.

"We tried to lead cheers for the team, not just perform," explains the sprightly Loken who was an active part of the tradition from 1947 through 1983.

"All those Michigan fans are packed into that stadium and their emotions want to come out. We tried to follow the crowd, not neces-sarily lead them. They're ready to respond. We were doing what all of them felt inside."

From Crisler to Oosterbaan to Elliott to Bo, Loken and his crew pumped plenty of life into the students, alumni, faculty and a variety of Wolverine loyalists.

"I loved those old Friday night pep rallies," Loken recalls. They were held mostly in front of the graduate library and sometimes where Ferry Field used to stand.

"I had the pleasure of introducing Bo at some of them. He was one of the most inspiring speakers I've ever heard. He could really turn a crowd on."

Before anyone took the microphone at the

"It must have been a Friday in front of the Michigan Union."

Newt Loken and the cheerleaders—part of the romance of Michigan Football.

rallies, the speaker was told to roll up his pant legs.

"Roll 'em up...roll 'em up," the crowd would yell. "It was just an old tradition to spice things up."

Loken's squads started the tradition of doing a backflip off the rail of the wall that surrounds the stadium for each point Michigan scored. By the time the Wolverines had finished running up some scores, the squad got a little dizzy.

When Loken arrived at Michigan after World War II, the cheerleading squad consisted of eight to ten members of the men's gymnastics team. It wasn't until early in the '70s that the team welcomed co-eds. Today the team consists of nine men and nine women. All have at least some gymnastics experience.

Loken still attends all the Michigan home games and particularly enjoys Homecoming.

"About 75 old-timers always come back to join the current team and the band on the field," he said. "It brings back a lot of warm memories."

The game, of course, is always the focal point of any Michigan Football Saturday. But the extras like the cheerleaders and band and tailgaters comprise the total Michigan experience.

"All those things bring life to the experience," Loken says. "They're all part of the romance."

"Times have changed for the better with the co-ed cheerleaders."

"We could have used that guy."

CANHAM'S PARTY

Don Canham didn't invent the tailgate party. But he made sure the University of Michigan was the first to market it. During Canham's tenure as Athletic Director, the spectacle of the Ann Arbor football Saturday assumed a life as colorful as the Wolverine team itself.

"I used to go to all the old Detroit Tigers' Opening Days," Canham reflected. "I always looked at Opening Day as a spectacle. There was something special about the atmosphere. I thought, at the time, if they only had space they could pitch a tent and have a ball.

"That's what I did when I became Athletic Director here. I pitched a tent and we had a ball. I knew that if we could find the space and do things right, people would do more than just walk into the stadium and then walk out."

Canham turned Michigan Football into a family affair. He made it friendly and entertaining for women and children.

"I knew a lot of women told their husbands, 'Saturday, we're taking the kids to the zoo,'" Canham said. "I wanted them to say, 'Saturday, we're taking the kids to Ann Arbor.'"

He did. He created an atmosphere. Somehow he blended the concept of an all-day family picnic with the mystique of the Michigan Football tradition. And it worked.

Canham's legacy to Michigan was to intro-

"Don Canham could sell suntan lotion at a hockey game. The man was that good."

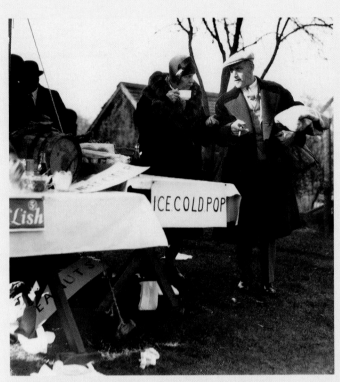

"Tailgating was a little less sophisticated but still a ritual back in the old days. At least the pop was cold."

duce modern business and marketing methods which actually pioneered a revolution in intercollegiate athletics.

Tailgate parties, which go way back to the early days of Michigan Football, comprise just one tentacle of the giant marketing octopus. Canham said that he and his team originally developed 60 different premium items bearing the famous Michigan mark. Today there are countless hundreds.

From pennants to T-shirts to jackets to caps to calendars to playing cards to cups and even to underwear, nothing escapes the marketing microscope that has helped to establish Michigan Football awareness among the best in the country.

And somehow it seems so appropriate for this revolution to have occurred at Michigan. Whereas Fielding Yost exercised the vision to construct a physical sports complex at least a half-century ahead of its time, Canham initiated

a similar vision of transforming football from four quarters on a Saturday afternoon into a year-long passion based on religious fervor.

Of course, marketing genius does not guarantee athletic success. Shelves of Michigan premiums might still be overstocked without the magnificence of Michigan Football dominance.

"The best decision I ever made came in December of 1968," Canham said. "If I hadn't hired Bo Schembechler, none of all the other stuff would have happened.

"Suppose I had hired somebody who had lost all those football games? What good would that have done me to promote? You can't fool the public. He gave us a product to promote."

Timing, of course, in any walk of life generally is the lifeblood of any long-lasting success.

Although certainly not as historically significant as the coupling of Lewis and Clark, the timing of Canham and Schembechler for Michigan was at least as critical as the first meeting between Mr. Procter and Mr. Gamble.

"Sure, Canham was a great promoter," Bo said. "Yes, he could sell the icicle to an Eskimo. He was, by far, the most influential athletic director in the Big Ten because he was so much smarter and had a better business sense.

"We've come a long way. The game now is an all-day affair."

"Looks like the old-time tailgaters used a dress code for their parties."

"What really made him a great athletic director, though, is that he always understood the fundamentals of a big-time college football program. He knew how tough it is to be the football coach at the University of Michigan. He wanted to give you everything you thought was necessary to win. He had a better feel for what an athletic director is supposed to be than anyone else. That's the difference. He was a coach's athletic director."

Mixing marketing genius with an inbred sense of coaching insight provided Canham with what Bo believes is "a helluva combination that was second to none."

"I remember that day I got hired, sitting with Don Canham and Bump Elliott. If we had a press conference today, there'd be 50 mikes in front of us."

Noticeable changes did not occur overnight. While Canham and his staff labored over various schemes to fill the nation's largest football stadium, Bo and his staff constructed their own program that propelled Michigan into a perennial national powerhouse.

When the two arrived in their eventual positions of power, Michigan was attracting crowds somewhere between 60 and 70 thousand. There were plenty of empty pews in the shrine of college football.

One of Canham's early attempts to fill the shrine almost backfired on the Michigan team.

To fill the stadium for the 1969 historic clash between unbeaten and No. 1 ranked Ohio State and underdog Michigan, which executed what many experts still regard as "the upset of the century," Canham allowed Ohio State to purchase 25,000 tickets for the game.

After Michigan's stunning 24-12 upset, the number of tickets offered to their enemy from Columbus was drastically reduced.

"Don't you ever do that to me again!" Bo told Canham. "From now on, they only get the same amount of tickets they offer us down there!"

Since then, it was hardly necessary to offer more than the mandatory number of tickets to any visiting foe.

The last time Michigan played before a home crowd of less than 100,000 was October 25, 1975, when a game with Indiana drew 93,857.

And it's not likely to happen again for a long, long time.

"Now the teams are so good and the population has increased so dramatically they're probably going to be sold out till the end of time," Canham said.

It's the game. It's the spectacle. It's the treasure of the Michigan Football tradition.

"If there's any item that doesn't have an 'M' on it today, there'll be one on it tomorrow."

"There used to be empty seats. Try finding some today."

PLAYING TO A FULL HOUSE

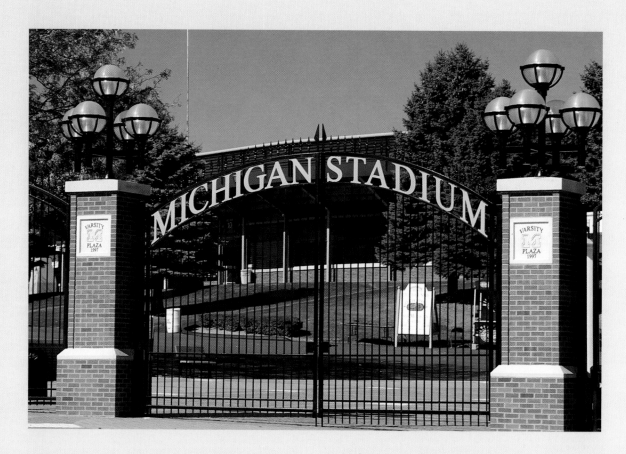

I t's "The Big House."

Size alone, however, incompletely paints all the romance, charm, and color of Michigan Stadium. The immensity of The Big House is complemented by its grandfatherly maturity.

Now in its eighth decade of existence, Michigan Stadium remains as vibrant today as the day it opened its gates on October 1, 1927.

No building, stadium, or any type of edifice is expected to retain that type of vitality.

Of course, Michigan Stadium is unlike any other facility in intercollegiate sports.

• There is the mystique of football's largest facility.

• There is the 100,000-person record for every home game since November 8, 1975.

• There are those inviting rustic red bricks and black iron fencing that captures a special collegiate charm from so many years ago.

• There is that singular thrill of walking into the stadium and being able to look down

"I love it. For fans and players, it's the best stadium in the country."

at one of the most meticulously manicured playing fields in America.

• There is Champions Plaza.

• There are rows of permanently inset inscribed bricks decorating the plaza from Michigan supporters.

• And there are countless millions of memories never to be forgotten from all the Michigan men and women who have proudly contributed to the Michigan Football tradition.

And it all goes back to Fielding H. Yost.

"A lot of people thought he was crazy at the time," said lifelong Ann Arbor resident Kip Taylor, who scored the first touchdown in The Big House.

"I think it was Mr. Yost who got the last laugh."

Everyone now shares a proud smile as the stadium stands as a monument to the most successful football program in intercollegiate history.

"When I took recruits into the tunnel, I used to tell them that if they thought football is a religion...you are now entering the greatest cathedral in the United States," said Jerry Hanlon, who served as an assistant throughout Bo's tenure. "It's hard to explain, but this stadium is unique. There are a lot of other pretty ones, but none have the aura or tradition that this one has."

Before the stadium opened, Michigan played its home games at Ferry Field, which was located where the Michigan outdoor track now stands. Prior to that, Michigan played at Regents Field.

Yost's vision for the finest athletic complex

in the country eventually persuaded the University to spend $240,000 on the land where the stadium now stands.

"There was nothing but a strawberry patch and a barn sitting on top of an underground spring," Taylor recalled. "I remember it well. Only Mr. Yost could have envisioned what it would become."

Yost imagined a day when Michigan football would demand seating for 130,000 people.

"He was so far ahead of his time," said Don Lund, who won nine varsity letters and later served as Associate Athletic Director. "He had the stadium built with double footings so it can easily be expanded. He knew people would get bigger so he had entrances built wider."

Yost didn't stop with the stadium. He built the nation's first athletic field house and intramural building. He also built one of the finest golf courses in the Midwest.

"When they dug dirt for the stadium, there

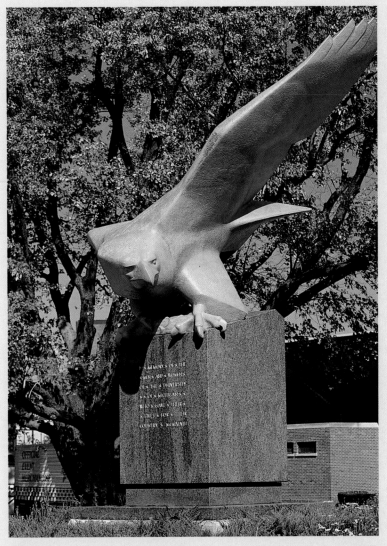

"The Eagle was dedicated in 1948 to the memory of the men and women of the University of Michigan who gave their lives for our country in World War II."

was this big hole in the ground," Taylor said. "There were springs, so there was water all over the place. Mr. Yost said, 'That's O.K... we'll just pipe it across the street and build a golf course.'"

And what a course it turned out to be! Yost hired legendary Alister MacKenzie to design it. Two of MacKenzie's other designs are the Augusta National and Cypress Point on the Monterey Peninsula.

But it's Michigan Stadium that remains as the "cathedral" for what all of college football represents.

With a seating capacity of 107,501 for the 1998 season, it's the largest football facility in intercollegiate athletics.

Size alone, however, comprises only part of the spirit of the Michigan Football tradition.

"How about this homecoming?"

"Here's the big hole that got it all started."

"Early on the stadium was almost flush with the level of the ground."

"Any time of day or any time of year, it's a piece of art."

RESPECT FROM THE IVORY TOWER

Now about 25 years later, Robben Fleming still smiles warmly when recalling one very special meeting with Bo.

For the former University of Michigan President, it remains one of his most precious memories from his 11-year association with "the ol' coach I still admire so much today."

Never one to wear his passion for Michigan and the University's proud football tradition anywhere but right out front where everyone could see it, Bo received a not so subtle message from the Big Ten Office.

"President Robben Fleming had a great understanding of intercollegiate athletics. We got along real well...except he thought I argued with the officials too much."

The Big Ten also respected Bo's zeal for the maize and blue. Officials there, however, requested quite forcefully that his actions on the sidelines be somewhat tempered.

President Fleming first contacted Athletic Director Don Canham.

"Don, we've got to get Bo to restrain himself on the sidelines," Fleming said. "I don't want him to get suspended and it's not good for his health."

"I got along well with all these men when they weren't wearing striped shirts."

It was decided Fleming would meet with Bo.

"I told him how much I respected his enthusiasm," Fleming said with a smile. "I did not want him to lose that because that's part of his very essence. But I asked him if maybe he could temper his reactions toward the referees."

Fleming and Bo shared a smile.

"I'll try," Bo said.

"And he did," Fleming said. "But he never lost that passion."

Bo also admired Fleming.

"He's an outstanding person and was an outstanding president," Bo said. "He understood the value of a superior athletic program to the University. He was a strong believer in letting the professionals run the program."

Under Canham and Bo, the athletic department and the football program was never a worry to Fleming.

"Look at that old 16-millimeter. Now the coaches have sophisticated million dollar taping equipment."

"Whenever you're dealing with a major university and there are a lot of overzealous alums and a variety of other tempting factors, there is the tendency for various recruiting violations," Fleming said. "I take great pride in the fact that we tolerated no hanky-panky. That always was most important to me."

Fleming remains proud of the fact that Michigan has managed to maintain a world-acclaimed academic program and a complementary athletic program second to none.

"I'm very concerned about kids receiving an education," he said. "What everyone must remember is the athletic life is quite short-lived.

"I'm opposed to some of the things I see in certain parts of the country. I can't understand why some coaches recruit young people who have no academic interest at all. That's wrong on the institution's part and also deceitful to the athlete."

Fleming is just as proud about the fact that Michigan takes great measures to ensure its academic interests and reputation.

"Michigan should be very proud of its excellence in both academics and athletics," he said. "I've always been a supporter of athletics. I grew up in a little town in Illinois hearing about that great passing combination of Benny Friedman to Bennie Oosterbaan.

Everyone dreaded playing Michigan. In the Big Ten, everyone realizes Michigan is always lurking out there."

Fleming's fondness for an upstanding college athletic program is precisely reflected in his admiration for Bo.

"Bo never stood for any sort of nonsense from his athletes," Fleming said. "He knew what was right. He taught them the right way. And he expected them to act in the right way. If they broke the rules, they did not play. I suspect there are hordes of former players who are thankful to him today for instilling those values."

Fleming served as President of the University from January 1, 1968 through January 1, 1979. He remains an active Michigan booster.

Still a resident of Ann Arbor, he attends all home football games and shares in the pageantry of a Michigan Football Saturday.

From Fleming's side of the desk, the Michigan Football tradition is as glorious as the view from the coach's side.

"Stick that yellow flag in your pocket!"

FROM CENTER TO THE WHITE HOUSE

"Gerald Ford is the only Michigan player to become President."

The Michigan Football tradition is rich with graduates who have succeeded in an eclectic collection of careers.

Of course, there have been a number of players who starred in the National Football League. Following a Hall of Fame career with the St. Louis Cardinals, Dan Dierdorf is a network television broadcaster. Jack Lousma never made it to the NFL, but he did make it to outer space as a United States astronaut.

"Even when he was President, Gerald Ford loved coming to our practices. He ate at our training table. He liked to get in the huddle. The problem was that there were always Secret Service agents around him. My players asked what they should do if the agents got in the way of a play. I told my men to run them over."

A good number of physicians, lawyers, educators, and international business leaders also matured through the program.

None, however, left his mark on world history as profoundly as a 1935 graduate who went on to become the 38th President of the United States of America.

Gerald Ford earned that distinction in 1974 after serving a short time as Vice President and several years as a leading Congressman in the House of Representatives.

He's the only former President to have played on two national championship teams (1932-1933). In 1934 he was named Michigan's Most Valuable Player as a center.

"Even before I went to Michigan, I felt there was something very special and wonderful about its tradition," he said. "It's vibrant, stimulating, and has a certain wholesomeness. I've retained that feeling throughout my life and remain very loyal to the program. I follow all of Michigan's fortunes quite closely. It's impossible not to have been imbued by that long tradition of Yost and Crisler and Schembechler."

President Ford played under Coach Harry Kipke. During Mr. Ford's first two varsity seasons, the Wolverines posted a 15-0-1 record.

In his senior year, they fell to 1-7. Of course, no other 1-7 team in history had a center who went on to become President of the United States.

"Some of the lessons I learned from competition on the football field were as valuable as any that I learned in the classroom," he said. "The concept of teamwork has always been particularly impressed upon all Michigan teams."

As with all former Michigan football players, President Ford fondly recalls how the University's present was always touched by its proud past.

"When I played, Fielding Yost was the Athletic Director," he said. "He was truly a living legend. I remember him coming around to our practices. That hat of his was always half-cocked on his head. He never smoked it, but he always was chewing on a cigar."

President Ford has been a frequent visitor to his school's games and even some practices.

During halftime of the Michigan State game, on October 8, 1994, President Ford's No. 48 was retired. It is one of just five numbers to have been retired by the University.

No. 48 from the Class of 1935 not only left his mark on Michigan tradition, but also on American history.

UP FROM THE TRENCHES

"He's going to be a great A.D."

Tom Goss had only been in the job of Athletic Director for a couple of months when he joined his team in celebration of the National Championship after Michigan whipped Washington State in the 1998 Rose Bowl.

"It was wild and very special," Goss said. "Hearing the seniors talk about going out a winner and being a 'Michigan Man' was particularly moving."

That feeling of becoming a "Michigan Man" has stayed close to his heart since Goss played on the line from 1966 through 1968. He wears it as openly as sunshine on a hot July afternoon.

"It's not something like water in a bottle

where you drink it and you become a 'Michigan Man,'" Goss said. "It's something you earn.

"It's tradition. You see history and consistency here and you feel good. Whether it's winning championships or helping each other to become 'Michigan Men,' there's no other feeling like it."

Goss played on the last three teams of Coach Bump Elliott. He vividly recalls mingling with Michigan legends who always were present.

"When I was getting ready to graduate, Bennie Oosterbaan called me into his office," Goss said. "He said, 'I'm going to make six calls.' I wound up getting six interviews and six job offers at some very fine companies. That's what Michigan is about."

That's the feeling Goss never wants to lose. Not for the current student-athletes who are learning to become "Michigan Men" and not for those in the future who will get that opportunity.

Shortly after graduating in 1968, Goss received first-hand experience of looking for prospective "Michigan Men." It occurred before NCAA rule changes prohibited alumni from helping to recruit high school athletes.

"When Bo got here, he needed a little help recruiting in Detroit and I was happy to help," Goss said. "At one time there were 11 kids here that I'm proud to say I helped to recruit.

"Bo made one thing very clear. No matter how much talent a young man had, Bo never wanted that kid unless that kid wanted Michigan even more. He never dealt under the table. If a kid was looking for something extra, Bo had a simple message — WALK... we don't want you."

That says it all. It's the essence of the "Michigan Man."

It's also the reason why Bo remains so close to Goss's heart.

"Bo is the yardstick I use for defining honesty, integrity, trust, and courage," Goss said.

Goss sees striking similarities between Bo and Coach Lloyd Carr.

"Certainly they have totally different personalities," Goss said. "But underneath, they're pretty much alike. With Bo, his No.1 priority was always his players. His No. 2 priority was his former players. That's the same way Carr is.

"When you have quality coaches like Carr and the staff he has assembled, you can win with above-average talent even if they aren't the best."

That is, of course, if those players are "Michigan Men."

Goss attacks the challenges of his position with the same energy he attacked opponents when he wore the winged helmet three decades ago.

"I've been entrusted with the direction of something that is very dear to the hearts of so many good people," Goss said. "I must make sure to manage it properly."

The Michigan tradition casts a longer shadow than perhaps most people realize.

"Former players from 10, 20, 30 even 50 years ago still come around and remain as enthusiastic about the University as when they were here," Goss said. "I listen to what they say and appreciate the tradition that we all uphold. I'm a firm believer that success of the future is based on the success of the past."

There is no more glorious past than that which Michigan enjoys. Under the leadership of men such as Goss, the future looks equally bright.

KEEPER OF HELMETS AND SECRETS GALORE

Jon Falk is like one of those hundreds of helmets for which he's responsible.

It's easy to take a helmet for granted. But no one is fool enough to play a game without one.

Falk is the Michigan Football Equipment Manager. He's responsible for all the equipment and facilities. With about 110 players during the heat of a season, the job can be unnerving.

For instance, Falk oversees the distribution and upkeep of nearly 2,000 pairs of shoes and 300 of those celebrated winged-tip helmets. Each day during the season, he and his crew wash about 800 pounds of uniforms, towels, and miscellaneous equipment.

In any collegiate or professional sport, few are privy to all the little secrets of a program as is the equipment manager. It's the nature of the position. They arrive long before any of the players and still are there after they've gone. Any tricky problem can usually be solved by the equipment manager.

Falk has held the Michigan head job since 1974. There's an unwritten rule in sports that certain stories never leave the locker room. Some experiences, though, make the long hours all worthwhile.

There was that frigid January evening in 1985 when, driving down I-94, Falk spotted a frozen figure hitchhiking on the shoulder. He thought the hat on the figure looked curiously like that of Bo's. The stalled car also resembled that of the coach.

"Jon Falk is one of the best equipment managers in the country. He does a great job with the equipment and a great job with the players...as long as he doesn't try to coach too much."

Falk pulled over and sure enough...there was Bo.

"He was caked with ice," Falk recalled. "His hands were, literally, shaking."

"Where are you going?" Bo asked his equipment manager.

"Henry Hatch (third from left) was a legend at Michigan. Bill Freehan (second from left) could have been a good one here. But he did all right with the Detroit Tigers."

"They come and they go."

Falk's position provides a unique perspective on the coaches he serves. Although he concedes their personalities are different, Falk sees striking similarities between Bo and Lloyd Carr.

"I told Lloyd there's a lot of Bo in him," Falk said. "Bo was tough and no nonsense. There was nothing more important to Bo than his players. He demanded the best for all of them, even those who didn't play.

"Bo always recruited the kids who had character along with talent. It's the same thing Lloyd does. Those are the kind of kids who can be coached and turned into champions. Those are the kids that Michigan wants."

"Well, Bo, I sort of had plans," Falk answered.

"Well, you've got new plans now," Bo said as Falk drove him home.

After thawing a little, Bo told Falk that three state police cars had passed while he was thumbing a ride.

"Well, Bo, we did finish 6-6 last year," Falk cracked.

Bo not only respected Falk's professionalism over the years, but enjoyed having him around.

After a press conference at which Bo announced he was stepping down as coach, he went to his usual locker in the coaches' room to prepare for a personal workout. It's always been Falk's policy to clear a locker as soon as someone leaves.

When Bo got to his, it was cleaner than Old Mother Hubbard's cupboard.

"Falk," Bo shouted. "You've got me cleaned out already?"

"They come and they go, Hobbs," Falk said, borrowing a line from *The Natural*.

"Look at those old-timers turn out those football shoes. We had them long before Nike came along."

"Ticket Director Don Weir used to count them by hand."

"I hope that guy gets lucky."

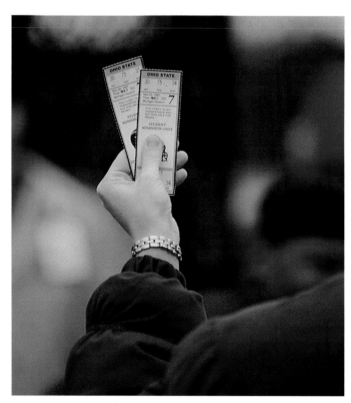

"This guy's got to be crazy to sell those two."

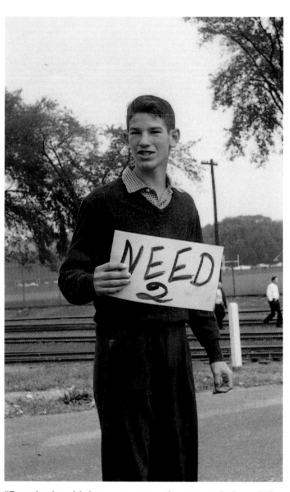

"Even in the old days, someone always needed a pair."

"You couldn't speak at a pep rally if you didn't 'roll them up.'"

"Now that's getting down and dirty for the team in the old Mud Bowl."

"That's the train station back in the '30s (now the Gandy Dancer) and they're waiting for the Michigan team."

"Those people are waiting for the 1997 National Champions."

"I love his enthusiasm, but I hope his mother doesn't recognize him."

"Roads were a little more narrow back then, but they all led to a good old-fashioned football game."

"They're all coming to the Big House. That's the kind of traffic jam I like to see."

"That old golf course has seen a lot of different car models over the years."

"A young entrepreneur."

"By car, by rail, by bus...everyone wants to get to a Michigan game."

"The early days of crowd control."

HOME SWEET HOME

Before the Big House, there was football at Michigan. In fact, the Wolverines had a few homes before Michigan Stadium opened in 1927.

From 1883 through 1892, Michigan played its home games at fields in Ann Arbor and Detroit. In 1893, "The Athletic Field," later known as Regents Field, opened with seating for 400 fans. With the erection of temporary bleachers to accommodate up to 17,000, the Wolverines compiled an impressive 87-2-3 record in all games at Regents Field.

In 1902, the name of the complex was changed to Ferry Field in honor of Detroit native Dexter Ferry who donated 21 acres. In 1906, the Wolverines moved to a new site on that donated land, located where the Michigan outdoor track now stands.

A maze of hash marks speckled Ferry Field. From 1903 until 1912, a team had three downs to advance the ball five yards toward the goal (increased to 10 yards in 1906). The first player to receive the ball had to cross the scrimmage line at least five yards left or right of where the ball was put into play.

In 1914, concrete stands increased the capacity of Ferry Field to 25,000 and in 1921, expansion stretched it to 40,000.

Then along came the Big House.

In 1925, the land where Michigan Stadium stands was purchased for $240,000. The Michigan Board of Athletics offered bonds at a price of $500 each to pay for stadium construction.

At a cost of $950,000, the stadium opened in 1927 with a structure housing 70 rows designed for 72,000 fans. With the addition of wooden bleachers, it hosted 84,401. Increased capacity continues right to the present as the Big House reigns as king of all football.

"They had aerial shots even back then."

"Look at those hats on the boys cramming into Ferry Field."

"That's Ferry Field at the 1904 University of Chicago game. Have you ever seen so many hash marks in your life?"

I remember the stand at Thermopylae
The Greek Guard made one day;
I remember the legions that Caesar used
To shatter the Gallic sway;
And I remember across the years
Two banners that crowned the crest,
When Yale was king of the conquered East,
And Michigan ruled the West.

At night in my humble den I dream
Of the glories that used to be–
Of Hannibal taking the Alpine Trail,
Of Drake on the open sea;
And then I wander the ancient ways
To dream a dream I love the best,
When Yale was king of the conquered East,
And Michigan ruled the West.

—Grantland Rice

"Doc Losh taught Astronomy at Michigan forever. She never missed a game. She had her own grading system — A for Athletes, B for Boys and C for Co-eds. There wasn't a guy who didn't love her."

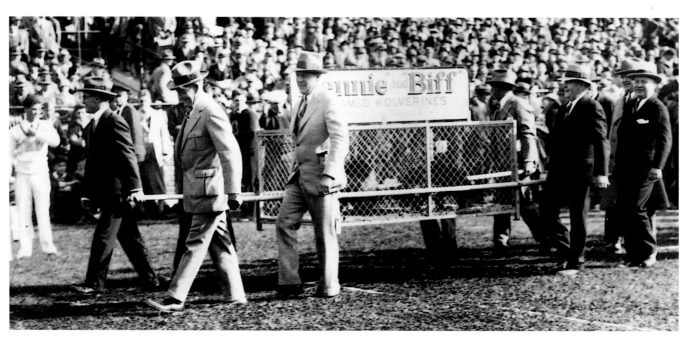

"The wolverine is the meanest animal of its size in the world — just like the men who wear the Maize and Blue."

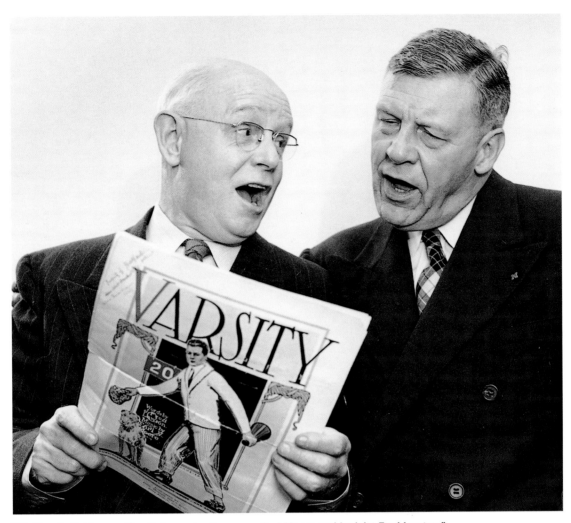

"Michigan's fight song 'Varsity' sung by Composer Earl Moore and Lyricist Fred Lawton."

"'Little Dog Blue' used to run a quick 40 and got a lot of laughs during half-times back in the '70s."

"Father Alex Miller marched in the Alumni Band. That's tradition. He has two great loves — St. Andrew's Episcopal Church and University of Michigan Football."

"You better get ready for kickoff now."

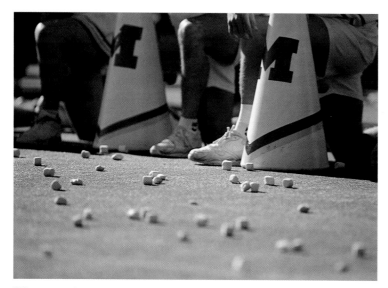

"Those are the only marshmallows we want on that field!"

"Now that's what I call spirit."

GO BLUE GO

"The sign is a Michigan tradition. It started long before I got here and is still practiced. Before we take the field for every game—home and road—every player and coach touches this sign."

"Even at the Great Wall of China, you can find a 'Michigan Man.'"

"Even at practice, I liked our players to hit and get hit. But no one was allowed to touch anyone in a red shirt. We couldn't afford to lose Mike Taylor or Elvis Grbac."

AND IF YOU'RE STRONG ENOUGH TO STAY...

Those Who Stay Will Be Champions.

— Bo Schembechler

 o one involved with Michigan Football will ever forget spring practice my first year here in 1969.

We inherited a good team. They had gone 8-2 the year before.

But one of those losses was brutal. They were humiliated at Ohio State, 50-14. There's no question that, at that time, Ohio State had the best team in college football...arguably the best ever.

At Michigan, we just couldn't let that happen.

The Michigan team had a lot of talent. We made it our goal to make that team TOUGH.

We had to take that talent and make it MEAN. I wanted them so mean that they'd scare themselves when they bumped into each other.

NO-body was going to out-hit us. NO-body was going to out-hustle us. If we got beat, it was because the other team on that day played a little better than we did. No team, though, was ever going to out-work us.

NO TEAM!

That spring practice was hell for all those players. I mean a true living hell. We had a lot of attrition.

That's when I put up a sign that hung over my office over the years — "Those Who Stay Will Be Champions."

The sign cost $300. At the time, that was a lot of money for a sign. Don Canham really got upset. It was a beautiful sign, though.

When Canham got the bill he called me immediately. "Schembechler...what the hell is this?" he screamed. "We need that sign," I said. "Don't worry."

We wanted commitment. We told those players that if they made a commitment, they'd become champions.

All those young men who stayed did become champions. And so did the ones after them. And the ones

THOSE WHO STAY WILL BE CHAMPIONS

after them.

That's what Michigan Football is about — CHAMPIONS.

Players make championships. Not just players who have talent. Talent alone is a good start.

Champions, though, are carved out of character. Without character, talent can be beaten.

Give me a good team with players full of character and I'll take them over a great team with no character.

Michigan football builds character. In the long run, character always wins.

We hear about all the All-American players. They get the headlines. They deserve them. Their names will live forever. Guys like...Mandich...Dierdorf...McKenzie...Carter...Leach...Howard...Woodson. Over the years, we've been blessed with several at Michigan.

But I'm just as proud of every young man who put on that Michigan uniform and stuck it out for four years even when he didn't have a chance to play a game.

A lot of guys come here thinking they're going to have a great playing career. All of a sudden they discover there are two or three players at their position who are just a little bit bigger and a little bit quicker.

But these guys show up for practice day after day. They suit up for the demonstration team. They get bruised and bloodied and beat up. Their only chance to play is in some lopsided game.

They don't complain, though. They just grind it out.

When they graduate, people think they didn't have such a good career.

I think they had a GREAT career. They showed character. Michigan Football is all about character. We could not have won without each and every one of them.

That's why I changed the rules for winning a Michigan letter. It used to be based on the amount of time played.

"That's the 1902 Rose Bowl. And Michigan was there!"

Weeks. Shorts, Snow, Heston, Herrnstein

TACKLE-BACK-RIGHT PLAY.

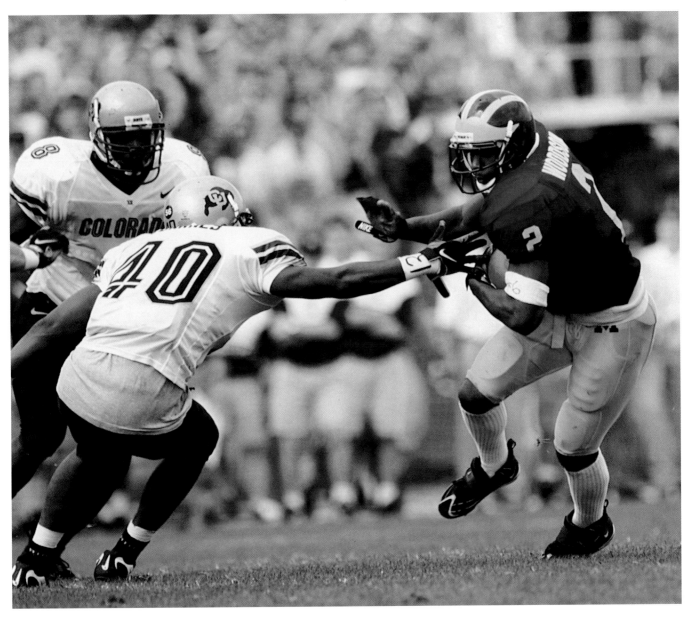

For me, if a young man came out to practice every day for four years...if he hustled...if he sweat...if he bled...then he earned a letter the same as any player who started every game.

Most of these guys go out and make something of their lives. They understand the most important lesson Michigan Football can teach — the only way to individual success is through the success of a team.

They don't learn that from a book. They don't learn that in a classroom. They learn it from Michigan Football.

And they carry that lesson for the rest of their lives.

Jimmy Hackett was one of those guys. He was our demonstration team center in 1976. Today he's the president of the Steelcase Company. That's the largest manufacturer of office furniture in the world.

Not so long ago, I told Jimmy how proud I am of him.

"Coach," he told me, "I run this company exactly the way you ran Michigan

"Look at Charles Woodson slip through all those defenders."

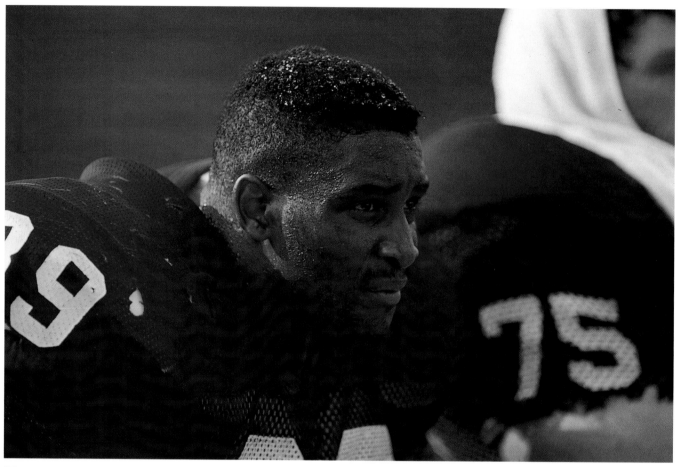

"That's sweat. That's Michigan. That's Derrick Walker."

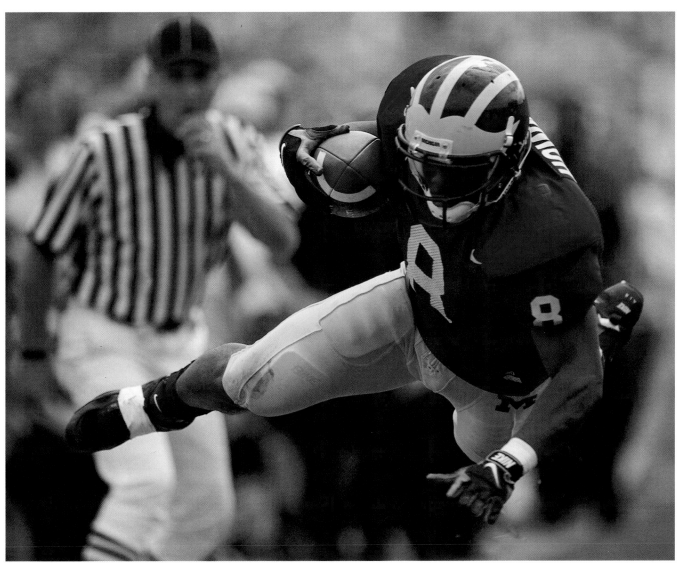

"Chris Howard did everything for that one extra yard."

"Even on the sidelines, everybody stays in the game."

Football. Any man who works here — all 12,000 — who wants an appointment with me gets it."

Hackett was our third-team center. And when he wanted to talk to me, all he had to do was come to the office. Or pick up the phone. He meant just as much to me as the starting quarterback. Jimmy remembers that.

"You can't see all those guys," I said.

"Coach, I can work everybody in," he said. "It doesn't take up my whole day. And I'll tell you one thing — after talking to the guys in the plant, I know more about what's going on than I do from all the guys who surround me in the executive suite."

I had a rule. I never wanted to be interrupted during a meeting — unless a player wanted to talk to me.

I don't care if I was talking to the president of the university or if I was in the middle of a television interview. And it didn't matter if the player was an All-American senior or the 125th man on the team.

"Jimmy Hackett didn't get to play much, but he made a great contribution to our success."

If that young man wanted to talk to me, then he got the time. He might have been in some kind of trouble. It might have taken a lot of courage to tell me something. If I tell him to come back in a couple of hours, he might never come back.

That's just not RIGHT.

That's the way you build a team. Every one of those 125 players is part of that team.

I never lied to them and I never expected them to lie to me. That's all part of building a team with integrity. That's all part of Michigan Football.

One of the greatest success stories of my career involved a player who had no business even coming out for the team.

This guy had no chance to play. NONE!

He wound up playing middle guard on our undefeated 1973 team. Now he's gone on to become an executive at the Ford Motor Company.

In the summer of 1970, I was sitting in my office when this incoming freshman asked my secretary if he could see me.

"Coach Schembechler, my name is Don Warner," he said. "I've been admitted to the school of Engineering. I'm here for orientation and I want to come out for football."

He was about 5-foot-10, 175-pounds and a cocky little son of a gun. I figured he had to be a halfback who still needed to put on a few pounds to keep from becoming a pancake.

"You do?" I said. "What position do you play?"

"Offensive guard," he shot back.

Now I'm getting a little amused.

"Where did you go to school?" I asked him.

He said he had graduated from Dearborn Divine Child.

I had visited Divine Child. They had four real fine players the previous year who were recruited to Division I schools.

"I've seen Divine Child," I told him. "I don't remember you.

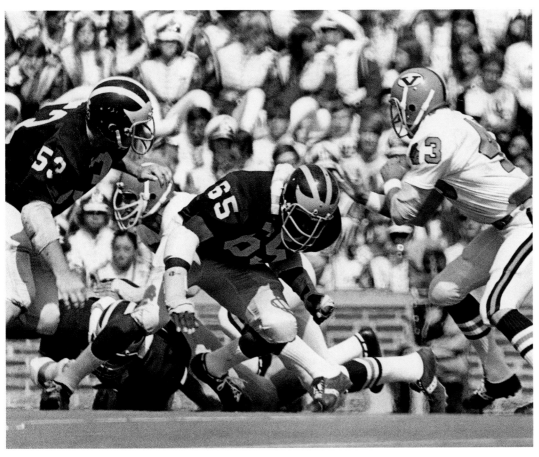

"Do not mess with No. 65. THAT'S Mr. McKenzie."

And besides, do you know who plays offensive guard here at Michigan? We've got Reggie McKenzie at 6-5 and 265 pounds. We've got Tom Coyle at 6-3 and 260 pounds. Now where in the heck are you going to fit in?"

He looked me in the eye. He never flinched.

"O.K.," he said. "If I'm too small to play offensive guard, I'll play middle guard on defense."

Now he's got me going.

"If you play middle guard, McKenzie and Coyle are the guys who are going to knock you from one side of the field to the other," I said. "I'm not going to let you come out. You're wasting our time. More important than that, you're going to get killed."

He still didn't flinch. He reminded me that I had spoken at the Divine Child football banquet.

"You told us that if we make up our minds to do something, never let anyone talk us out of it," he said.

Now he's really got me going.

"Why you little smart aleck kid," I said. "I'll tell you what I'm going to do. I'm going to let you come out. But as soon as you find out that you're not big enough to handle it, you quit. And I'll never look at you as a quitter because you showed me something just to go out there in the first place."

He thanked me and promised he'd never quit.

"If Reggie didn't get you, then Tom Coyle (60) did."

"Donnie (54) was a little short on size but awfully big on heart."

That whole first year he came out to practice every day. We put him on the demonstration team for the last four or five plays of the day and those big guys knocked him all the way to Ypsilanti.

At the end of the season, I called Donnie into my office just like I talked to every player.

"I don't know how you did it, but you stayed out there the whole season and I admire you," I told him. "But you realize now that you're too small to play here."

Just like he did at the beginning of the season, he never flinched.

"No, Coach," he said. "I know what I have to do. I'm going to lift weights, get bigger, and be out here next spring."

He came back the next year...and the next. He was playing on the demonstration team his junior year and actually started to stop some of the plays we were practicing.

"If we can't block Warner, how in the heck are we going to win Saturday?" I asked my coaches.

Finally in spring practice before his senior year, he's still out there. He was about 195 pounds by then and quick as a cat. Our first two middle guards had graduated. I told our coaches to put Warner No. 1 on the depth chart. I figured one of our young players would beat him out in the fall.

Well, let me tell you something. He came out that next fall and made up his mind that NOBODY was going to beat him out.

He had a mind like a computer. He studied the moves of every player. He knew when they were going to move to their left or move to their right. He knew when a guard was going to block for a run or drop back to protect on a pass.

"Dennis Franklin's winning percentage at Michigan was greater than any quarterback in history and he never got a chance to play in a Rose Bowl. We fixed that rule!"

He started every game that 1973 season and we went into the Ohio State showdown undefeated. During the week between classes, Warner was in the projection room all the time. He studied every film of the season on Ohio State.

On the Thursday before the game, I walked out of my office to use the men's room and happened to run into Warner.

"I want you to know, Coach, I studied every film," he told me. "I got their center down cold. He's the best one we've played. Don't worry, though. I know when he's going left and I know when he's going right. I know the splits between the guards. I know what I have to do.

"No one man can block me. When they put two men on me, you get the linebacker to scrape into the hole. If we stop their run, we are going to win because they can't beat us passing."

I just stood there and listened to him talk.

"I'm glad I ran into you," I said.

At the end of the first half that Saturday, we were down, 10-0. Our whole defense was madder than a wild bull. They all were shouting — "Just score 11 and we'll win. They'll never score another point!"

Sure enough, in the second half we scored 10 and finished in a tie.

In the fourth quarter in the series before our quarterback, Dennis Franklin, went down with a broken collarbone, Warner went down with a knee injury. They had to help him off the field.

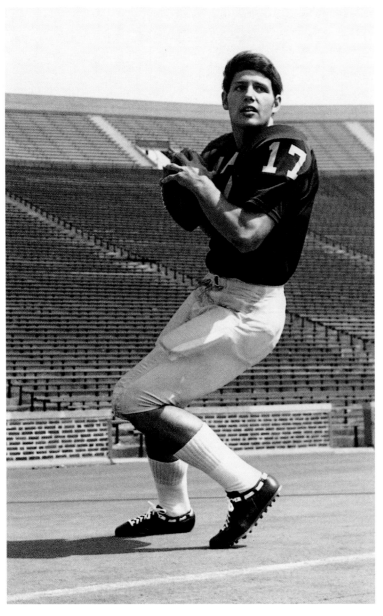

"Now it's Dr. Tom Slade."

For four years I thought he was going to get killed. And this was the first time he ever got hurt enough to come out of a game or even a practice.

Dr. O'Connor drove both players to the hospital. Warner's career was finished. He was going to have surgery the next day. Warner was sitting in the back of the car with his leg stretched out across the seat.

"Denny, don't worry," he said to Franklin. "When we go to the Rose Bowl, Larry Cipa will do a great job substituting for you. But who in the hell are we going to get to play middle guard?"

That was Donnie Warner. He was a kid who had no business playing here and wound up starting for an undefeated team...on sheer guts and determination.

THAT is Michigan Football!

Tom Slade was another kid who never knew how to quit. In 1971 he was our starting quarterback. The next year he got beat out by Dennis Franklin.

I told Slade that he would be holding on kicks and playing back-up. He never gave up. He came out and worked hard every day as if he was still starting. He learned a lot from his experience in Michigan Football. Today he's my dentist.

This is all part of the Michigan Football tradition. It goes all the way back to Yost to Crisler to Carr today.

That's why every time Michigan Football takes a bad rap, I take it personally. All the coaches, all the players, and all the fans do.

The Michigan Football tradition is filled with character. It's the heart of the program. And character isn't restricted only to All-Americans. Just ask Donnie Warner.

THIS MAGIC MOMENT

Kip Taylor doesn't mind being a treasured piece of trivia in the fabled history of Michigan Football.

In fact, he's proud of his little niche that no one else can share.

The year was 1927. Babe Ruth dominated the American sports scene by blasting 60 home runs for the New York Yankees. In Ann Arbor, Fielding Yost opened Michigan Stadium — seven decades later still the shrine of major college football.

The date was October 1st and Michigan crushed Ohio Wesleyan, 33-0.

Taylor was a sophomore end for the Wolverines. In his first varsity game before 17,877 persons, Taylor scored the first touchdown in Michigan Stadium history.

It was one of those magic moments in time. Taylor's eyes still sparkle just thinking about it. Now ninety years old and still residing in Ann Arbor, reliving the moment makes it feel as though it happened only last week.

"Bennie Oosterbaan was the other end," Taylor said. "He was a three-time All-American so they were covering him pretty tight. I went back to the huddle and said that I was wide open. I went out and got open again. Louis Gilbert hit me with a 28-yard pass and we were on the board. The rest is history."

Once in a while, Taylor still finds his way over to Michigan Stadium. He watches most of the games on television and still gets as nervous as when he was performing on the field.

"I sit there and bite my nails," he said. "There's nothing in college sports that matches Michigan Football. Who ever

#619

thought it would get to be 105,000 people every Saturday with people coming to town the night before? I love it."

Taylor said he "still gets chills" thinking about his magic moment in history from 71 years ago. So many other great ones have followed. This one, however, is forever locked in time.

CALLING A CHOSEN FEW

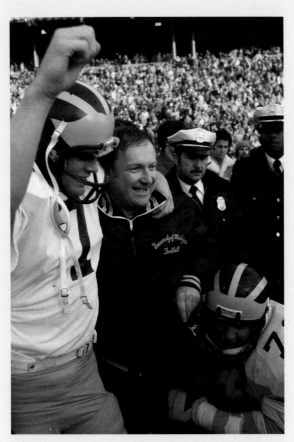

"You've got to recruit them and you've got to coach them. Rick Leach was a leader for Michigan for four straight years."

Over the years, college football recruiting has undergone more face-lifts than the Gabor sisters.

In spite of myriad changes, there remains at least one constant.

Recruiters for the University of Michigan are always welcomed through the front door.

"When I recruited for Michigan, I never went into a house through the back door," said long-time Bo assistant Jerry Hanlon.

"When you recruit for Michigan, you not only represent an outstanding football program, but also a university which the parents and high school teachers all want their kids to be associated with."

Although the annual recruiting war for the nation's finest high school prospects has bitterly intensified, Michigan's arsenal of weapons could fill a whole section of "The Big House." Some include:

• Tradition — the opportunity to play for a team that is nationally ranked annually.

• Coaching — one of the most dedicated all-around coaching staffs in the country.

• Stadium — not only the largest, but also the most prestigious stadium in college football.

• Facilities — with Schembechler Hall and the indoor practice field, the model for intercollegiate excellence.

• Education — the University tops most lists of public institutions in the United States.

"There are a lot of fine schools and a lot of very good football programs around the country," Bo explains. "But when you combine all the factors, only one comes out on top — the University of Michigan."

Compared to today's highly intensified recruiting wars, the process of many years ago is somewhat like a typewriter in the modern world of high-tech computerization.

"Most good athletes from the state and around the Midwest just naturally wanted to go to Michigan," explained Don Lund, who won nine letters during his 1942-1944 varsity career.

"We must have put some points on the board."

"Mr. Yost or Fritz Crisler might send out a postcard saying they would like you to come to Michigan. A lot of the recruiting was done by local alumni groups. Probably the first time a recruit actually met the coach was in the fall on the field."

Lund graduated from Detroit's Southeastern High School in 1940. In addition to Michigan, he was recruited by Northwestern, Notre Dame, Michigan State, and Yale.

"In my senior year I attended the Michigan Football Bust and Tom Harmon had won the Heisman Trophy," Lund said. "I was so impressed by him and the entire Michigan program. That's when I knew I had to attend."

Competition now for the finest high school talent has assumed a life of its own. That's why the combined excellence of academics and athletics at Michigan is a nuclear weapon in the recruiting wars.

"If a kid wants a quality degree from a great university and also the chance to play for a nationally ranked team, that's a helluva combination to beat," Bo said.

"When you recruit and you go into a school or a home and say 'I'm from the University of Michigan,' you are always welcome. No one throws you out of there. And you always walk in the front door."

One of Bo's proudest recruiting efforts involved Stefan Humphries, an offensive guard out of St. Thomas Aquinas High School in Broward, FL. Humphries became a 1983 All-American. He also was awarded the Big Ten Conference's Medal of Honor for excellence in academics and athletics.

Before Humphries selected Michigan, it had been generally accepted that he would attend Notre Dame.

"I got to know the nun who ran St. Thomas

"Development and training have become a year-round process. Preparation is the key to success."

Aquinas real well," Bo said. "She was a helluva woman.

"She said, 'Bo, I don't want you coming down here and taking one of our kids away from Notre Dame.'

"I said, 'Sister, come on now. Notre Dame cannot give him the academics we can give. He wants biomedical engineering. How do you get that stuff at Notre Dame? He's got the grades to come here academically. You can't just base this decision on religion. We've got more than one Catholic Church in Ann Arbor. And I'll bet you I have as many Catholic players as Notre Dame does.'"

Bo persisted. He did not want to lose an outstanding young man. In an emotional press conference at the high school gymnasium, Humphries stunned a lot of so-called experts when he announced that he had chosen Michigan over Notre Dame.

"A few days later, the sister called me," Bo said. "She said, 'Now do I have tickets for the games up there?' She was a tremendous person."

Humphries also proved to be a tremendous individual. Not only was he a three-year starter, he eventually earned a medical degree.

"Michigan always has and always will recruit honestly," said Terrell Burton, who served as a longtime assistant under Bo. "We won't go under the table to get that one kid who might make the difference. But we'll win. And we'll win with integrity."

That same philosophy applies to today's program.

"Lloyd Carr and his whole staff have done a marvelous job," Bo said. "Look at the kids who make up the team. They're not just great football players. All these kids have excellent character. And every one of them plays for the team and the University of Michigan. That's the way it's supposed to be. That's the Michigan way!"

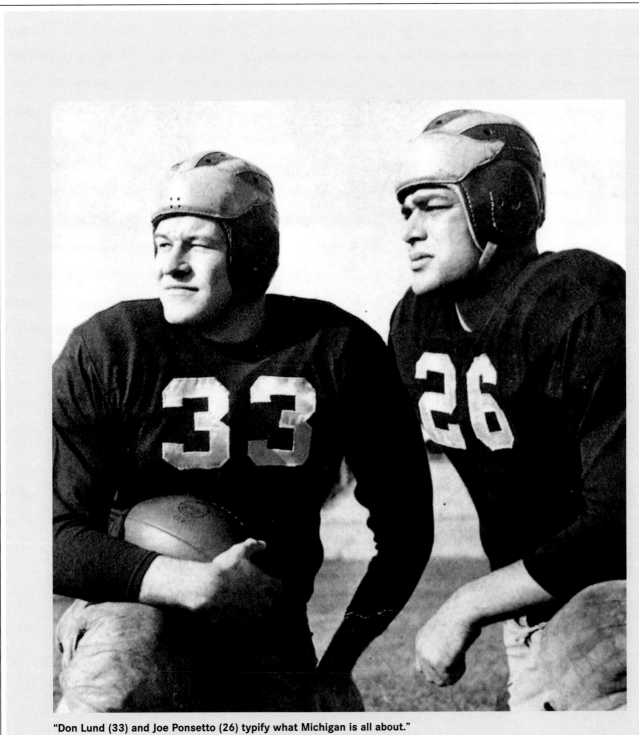

"Don Lund (33) and Joe Ponsetto (26) typify what Michigan is all about."

"Two great co-captains in 1983 — Stefan Humphries and John Lott."

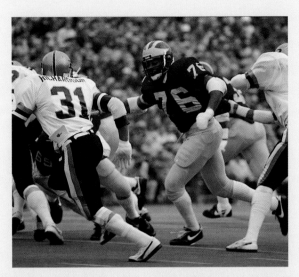

"Those white shirts want no part of Stefan Humphries."

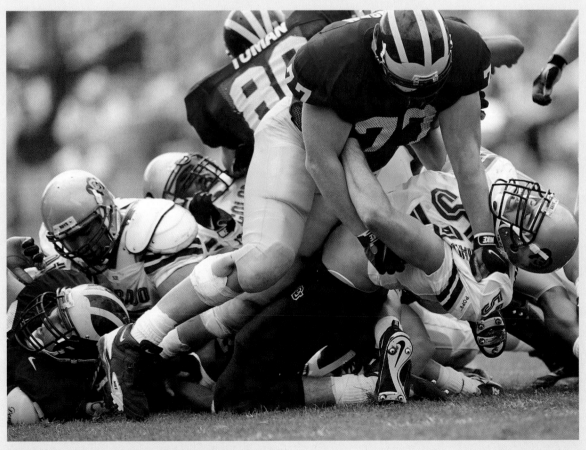

"At Michigan, that's what we call a pancake block."

PRICELESS MEMORIES

For Rick Leach, there are as many warm memories from his Michigan career as there are people who cram into that football stadium for each home game.

There should be, after spending four years (1975-1978) as the starting quarterback.

The warmest memory, though, occurred at the Ohio Stadium in Columbus on November 25, 1978 after Michigan defeated Ohio State, 14-3, for the third straight year.

After the usual postgame hysteria of beating the Buckeyes, Leach sat quietly in front of his locker. All of his physical strength had been left on the field. Except for the upcoming Rose Bowl, Leach had played his last game for Michigan. It was a bittersweet moment for the left-hander who established almost all of the school passing records.

Somehow, through the maze of celebrating supporters outside the Michigan locker room, his father, Richard, Sr., maneuvered his way into the room.

"I was drained...physically and mentally," Leach said. "I looked up and saw my dad walking toward me. When he got to my locker, we sort of looked at each other and then we hugged. Neither one of us said a word. We didn't have to. We communicated more than if we had said a thousand words."

The memory becomes even more precious to Leach with each passing year. That hard-fought victory marked the end of a remarkable four-year run. Both father and son quickly reflected on all the good times.

Leach's father and mother, Nancy, never missed one of their son's games. They still attend all home games and many on the road.

"Rick Leach started 48 consecutive games in four years, more than any other player in Michigan history. He could run that option and take a hit. I'll tell you — that man was tough!"

"Now that I have three sons of my own, I can only imagine the pride my father must have felt," Leach said. "That's something I'll keep for the rest of my life."

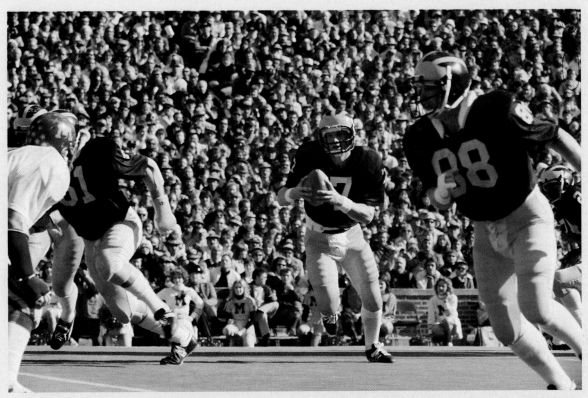

"That's Rick Leach running the option with Flint Southwestern High School teammate Gene Johnson leading the block."

The following spring, Leach became the Detroit Tigers' No. 1 draft pick. He spent nine years in the major leagues.

"When you're playing sports, you sort of get wrapped up in your own little world," he said. "Now that I'm part of the real world, I appreciate even more what the University of Michigan means to me.

"There's a special kind of chemistry and togetherness here. Everyone is part of it. It's not just the athletes. You hear people talk about the Michigan Family and all of it is true. The Michigan Family takes care of its own. It's a pretty good feeling to know that wherever you travel, there's always going to be part of that Michigan Family there to help you if you need it."

Leach left his mark on the Michigan record books. He was one of the finest athletes in university history. Three times he was named All-Big Ten quarterback. In 1978, he earned All-American honors and was named Michigan's and the Big Ten's Most Valuable Player. During his four years, the Wolverines shared three Big Ten championships and compiled an overall 38-8-2 record.

"Bo had such a passion for excellence and the tradition of Michigan Football," Leach said. "Of all the people I've met in sports, he was the greatest motivator I've ever been around. He knew how to get the best out of every player he had. He made you want to succeed. Those are the kinds of lessons that you carry throughout your whole life, even when your playing career is over."

Leach certainly made his coach proud. And the Michigan tradition is richer because of both of them.

EARLY MAIZE AND BLUE BLOOD

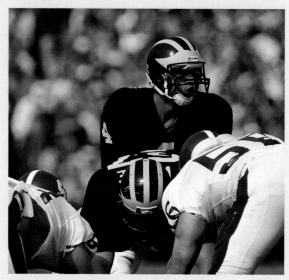

"And that's Jim Harbaugh — a leader of men!"

Jim Harbaugh is one of those special alums who has tasted all the plums of the Michigan Football tradition.

Before earning All-American honors as quarterback under Bo Schembechler and then going on to star in the National Football League, he grew up in Ann Arbor as a Michigan football fanatic. While his father, Jack, served as one of Bo's assistant coaches from 1972-1979, young Harbaugh went to all the practices starting at just nine-years-old, and served as a ball boy during the games.

"I lived and died with Michigan," Harbaugh said. "There's absolutely nothing on earth like a football Saturday in Ann Arbor. That's what I lived for.

"On Friday nights I never slept. I got so keyed up for the games. I listened to a Bob Ufer record over and over so much that I actually wore it out. I memorized all the words."

Former Michigan All-American quarterback Rick Leach was Harbaugh's boyhood hero.

Harbaugh spent his first two years of high school at Ann Arbor Pioneer. He spent his junior and senior years in California when his family moved there.

Harbaugh was recruited by Arizona and Wisconsin along with a variety of smaller schools. There was no decision to be made

"That's Jim Harbaugh when he was one of our ball boys! I must have kicked him out of a hundred practices."

once he was offered a scholarship from Michigan.

"I could never repay Michigan for everything it's done for me and my family," Harbaugh said. "Not just for the opportunity in football, but for everything it's meant to my life. Anyone who has gone to Michigan will tell you the same thing. You don't have to play football to realize that."

Harbaugh did play, though. And he played like few other quarterbacks in Michigan history.

A three-year starter (1984-1986), he earned All-American honors in his senior year. During that season he also was voted Michigan's Most Valuable Player, Big Ten Player of the Year, and finished third in the Heisman voting.

"I received such good coaching at Michigan," Harbaugh said. "From Bo and all the assistants. They taught us how to become men. To this day, whenever anything good or

bad happens to me in life I call Bo to get his feelings on the matter. He gets thousands of calls like that from his old players. I don't know if he truly understands how much he means to us."

That burning sense of Michigan tradition he felt as a player is still carried by Harbaugh today.

"When you play for Michigan, you can't help but feel all of the great players and coaches who performed before you," Harbaugh said. "That helped to give you a toughness for not letting them down. And no one ever wanted to let Bo down. He's the kind of person you wanted to do well for."

Harbaugh will never forget the speech Bo delivered to the team before the Wisconsin game in 1984.

"We beat Miami of Florida in the season opener and then got beat by Washington," Harbaugh recalled. "We played Wisconsin the next week. Before the game, Bo gave one of the best speeches I ever heard in my life.

"He said, 'People all over the country are saying that Michigan got MAN-handled by Washington. Can you imagine anyone MAN-handling Michigan? What do we tell guys like McKenzie and Dierdorf and all the guys who went before us?'"

Needless to say, Michigan went out that day and defeated Wisconsin.

Of all Harbaugh's Michigan football memories, one of his fondest came in 1985 after the Wolverines beat Ohio State, 27-17, in Michigan Stadium. After the game, Bo called Harbaugh into his office.

"'Do you realize how much you meant to Michigan today?'" he asked me. "'Do you realize how proud your parents are of you?' I'll never forget that moment."

Nor will Michigan fans ever forget what Harbaugh wove into the fabric of Michigan Football tradition.

ALL IN THE FAMILY

"Don Dufek set the table for his boys by winning the MVP of the 1951 Rose Bowl."

The Dufek family has permanently etched its name in the Michigan Football tradition.

Not once...not twice...but three times.

Don Dufek was a bruising fullback who scored both touchdowns and was named Most Valuable Player in Michigan's 14-6 victory over California in the 1950 Rose Bowl. Later he served as an assistant coach at Michigan.

Don, Jr. was an All-American strong safety and twice earned All-Big Ten honors. His brother, Bill, was a punishing offensive tackle who also was named to an All-Big Ten team.

Dufek played for Bennie Oosterbann. Both his sons played for Bo.

All three families still reside in Ann Arbor. And, of course, they attend all the football games.

"We park in the golf course and tailgate with everyone else," Bill said.

Few fathers have had the special football thrills that the senior Dufek has enjoyed.

"I feel very fortunate in a lot of ways," he said. "I was fortunate to play in a Rose Bowl in my senior year. Then I went to the Rose Bowl as an assistant coach, and that's the hardest because there's so much pressure. Then I got to go there when Billy played under Bo. And finally I went just as a fan. That's the easiest."

Both Dufek boys had to find out more about their father's Michigan heroics from others than they did from their dad.

"He's a very humble man," Bill said. "When my brother and I were kids, we used to wear his helmet and jersey that he got from All-Star games. But it wasn't till we played at Michigan that we found out from others how good he was."

Don, Jr. echoed his brother's feelings.

"One time the University wanted to display the trophy my dad won for being the MVP in the Rose Bowl," he said. "My father had forgotten where he had put it. It was stored away somewhere in the attic."

The Michigan Football tradition was felt by all the Dufeks.

"When I was growing up in Ann Arbor, those Saturdays were the biggest days of the year," Don, Jr. said. "You could buy end zone seats for $1. It was great."

"Billy and Donnie Dufek...when they hit somebody, that guy needed more than an umbrella to protect himself. This is at picture day, otherwise there would have been no umbrella. Mother Pat must have taken that photo."

Bill was always amused at other players when he participated in postseason All-Star games.

"Wherever I went, the guys always wanted to put on my Michigan helmet," he said.

Playing for Bo, the two young Dufeks learned how the Michigan Football tradition helped to mold them into men.

"Bo could take kids from every type of ethnic and social and economic background and mold them into one," Bill said. "I used to joke he treated everyone equally — like dogs.

"Honestly, though, I think Bo sort of symbolized the whole Michigan tradition. Everything is for the team. We've had our share of stars, but the whole experience is to produce excellence from teamwork."

The Dufeks certainly have left their mark on that tradition.

"That beat up nose on Don Dufek was a small price to pay for a victory in the 1951 Rose Bowl."

THE APPLE MAN

To some of the young Michigan players, he's first known as the "Apple Man."

There was a time when Bo was coaching when a couple of his younger men asked, "Who in the hell is the old guy who comes around with apples every Wednesday?"

"Take a look around this field," Bo told his players. "Who's wearing No. 87?"

After a quick look, they discovered no one was.

"That's because the number belongs to HIM," Bo said.

It's Ron Kramer — No. 87. The number was retired after his senior season in 1956.

"There used to be a man named Chestnut

"That's Kramer of Michigan!"

"Grab that ball, Kramer, and take it in for MICH-i-gan."

who brought apples around to us each week," Kramer said. "A while ago I decided maybe it was my turn."

So every Wednesday during the football season, Kramer picks up three bushels of apples — Michigan, of course — and delivers them to the football facility at Schembechler Hall.

He loves it. It gives him the chance to extend that tie to the happiest years of his life.

"There is absolutely no tradition like the Michigan tradition," Kramer says proudly. "A boy who comes here knows he is going to a high class educational institution and

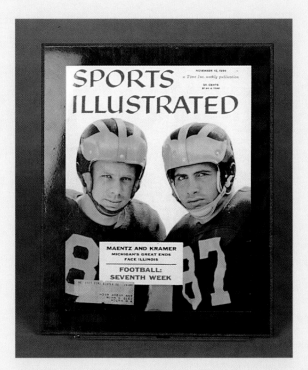

expects the athletic program to reflect those same standards. And he's never disappointed.

"It's impossible to put that feeling of tradition into words. You can't describe it. You feel it. I've been all over the world and there hasn't been a place where I didn't find a Michigan man.

"It's not a case of what the school can give you...it's what you can give back to the school."

Kramer gave back plenty. Not only did he achieve his degree, he also is rightfully regarded as one of the best all-around athletes in Michigan history.

He was a two-time football All-American. He played end on both sides of the ball and also spent time as running back, quarterback, punter, and placekicker.

Coach Bennie Oosterbaan described his blocking and tackling ability as the team's most valuable asset.

"To top off his marvelous physical gifts of size and speed and strength, plus an uncanny coordination, Kramer was one of the fiercest

competitors I've ever seen," Oosterbaan said. "Nothing was impossible for him — the impossible was only a challenge."

Kramer also captained the basketball team and was an accomplished high jumper in track. He finished his career with nine varsity letters when freshmen were ineligible.

Kramer's mother, the late Adeline, attended 241 straight Michigan home football games until she died in 1988. She held seats 24 and 25 in row 83 of section 2.

"Everybody knew her there," Kramer said. "It didn't matter if it was pouring rain or snowing, she never left till that game was over. She sat in row 83 — the number I wore for the Detroit Lions; she saw her last game in '87 — the number I wore at Michigan; and she died in '88 — the number I wore for the Green Bay Packers."

Kramer purchased a Michigan brick in his parents' honor near Champions Plaza. It reads — "John & Adeline Kramer, Parents of Ron Kramer."

It's impossible to touch the tradition of Michigan Football without conjuring up warm memories of Ron Kramer.

He still follows the games with the same passion he demonstrated on the field. And he cherishes his weekly Wednesday visits bearing Michigan apples to Schembechler Hall.

WISTERT...WISTERT... WISTERT

"Al Wistert...he didn't need a face mask."

The Wistert brothers didn't arrive at the University of Michigan wearing No. 11. All three did their part, though, to make it one of the most celebrated numbers in Michigan history. After they left, no one has worn it and no one ever will.

To honor the unprecedented piece of history the Wisterts contributed to the Michigan tradition, No. 11 has been retired.

Francis (Whitey), Albert (The Ox), and Alvin (Moose) all played tackle and all were voted first-team All-American, an accomplishment that has never been duplicated by three brothers on any level of collegiate competition.

The Wisterts came from Chicago. They were tougher than any midwestern snowstorm and played their position on the line as fiercely as a January blizzard.

"Whitey" paved the way by winning All-American honors for the 1933 Big Ten and

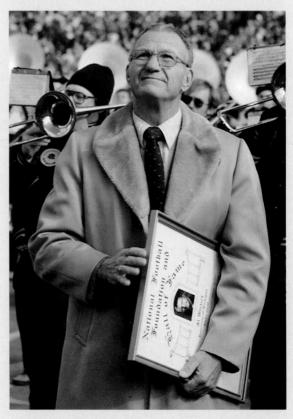

"Al Wistert never forgot his heart belongs to Michigan."

"What's better than one Wistert? How about three of them? From left to right: Alvin, Albert, and Francis."

National Championship team. He also was the 1934 Big Ten's Most Valuable Player in baseball and played professionally for Cincinnati.

"The Ox" earned his All-American honor in 1942 when he also was named Michigan's Most Valuable Player. He played nine years for the Philadelphia Eagles and eventually was selected to the National Football Hall of Fame.

"Moose" enjoyed as colorful a personal history as the Wisterts did collectively.

Not only did he not play high school athletics, he did not arrive at the University of Michigan until after serving four years in the Marines in World War II. After one year at Boston University, "Moose" came to Michigan in 1947. At 32, he was the oldest man ever to play for Michigan.

He earned All-American honors in both 1948 and 1949.

No. 11 belongs to the Wisterts. No one can take it from them.

HARMON OF MICHIGAN

I n the days of "Ol' 98," there was no contraption like the modern face mask.

It literally was "in-your-face football" and it took a lot of guts to go crashing through a line.

With his square jaw, needle nose, and eye for daylight, that's just the way Tom Harmon liked it. He was "Ol' 98" — Michigan's first

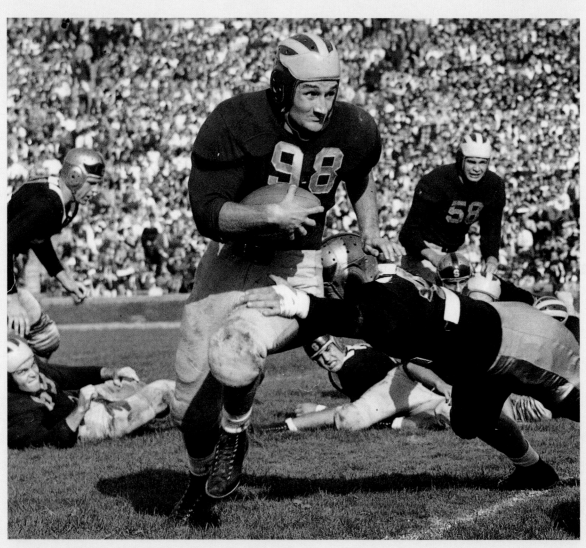

"Harmon of Michigan. No one will ever wear No. 98 again."

"That Heisman belongs to Tom Harmon, one of the greatest players in intercollegiate history."

Heisman Trophy winner and one of the nation's greatest backs of his era.

On the field there was nothing Harmon couldn't do. A two-time All-American halfback, he ran, passed, played defense, punted, and did the placekicking.

Twice he led the nation in scoring. For this three-year (1938-1940) career, Harmon ran and passed for 3,438 yards, threw 17 touchdown passes, kicked 33 extra points and two field goals, and scored 33 touchdowns.

In his Heisman season of 1940, Harmon saved the best for last. Before 73,480 fans at Columbus, he turned in one of the most magnificent individual performances ever by a Wolverine and left the field to a standing ovation even though Michigan crushed Ohio State, 40-0.

In that game, Harmon rushed for 139 yards and two touchdowns. He completed 11 of 12 passes for 151 yards and two touchdowns. He scored four extra points. He intercepted three

"There was NOTHING that man couldn't do."

"Harmon was a great triple threat player — run, pass and kick."

passes, including one for a touchdown. He averaged 50 yards per punt.

That game was a whole season for any other player. But then, Harmon never was just any other player.

Harmon came out of Gary, Indiana to become a Michigan legend and capture every Wolverine heart. The one that captured Harmon's heart was actress Elyse Knox, whom he married. Harmon settled in the Los Angeles area after playing professional foot-

ball and enjoyed a successful broadcast career.

An Air Force fighter and bomber pilot, he rose to the rank of Captain in World War II. Twice his plane was shot down and he walked back to safety. For his military heroics, he was awarded the Silver Star and Purple Heart.

No Michigan player will wear that retired number ever again. No Michigan fan ever will forget it.

"Ol' 98."

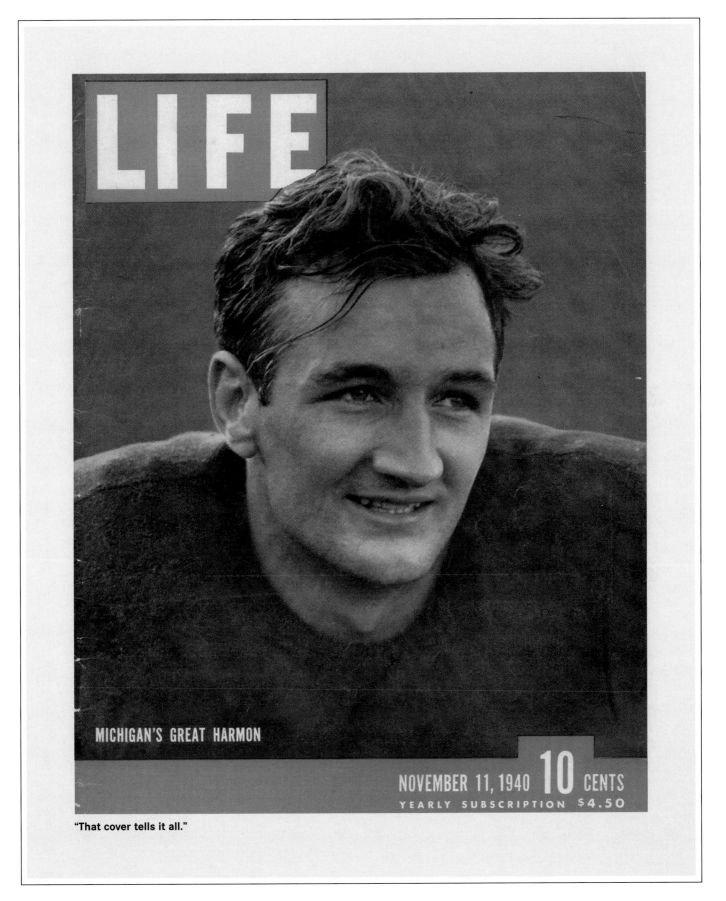

LIFE

MICHIGAN'S GREAT HARMON

NOVEMBER 11, 1940 **10** CENTS
YEARLY SUBSCRIPTION $4.50

"That cover tells it all."

STRIKE THE POSE

There were all those acrobatic catches just in the nick of time.

There was the time in the end zone after scoring a touchdown that he "struck the pose."

And always there was that infectious grin that sparkles so bright it makes everyone want to smile.

That was Desmond Howard, Michigan's second Heisman Trophy winner. Howard won the award after his All-American season in 1991.

Howard actually didn't just win it. He ran off with the voting as if he were racing for the end zone on another touchdown romp. He took the Heisman by the second largest margin of victory in the trophy's history.

There may have been better all-around players in Michigan history. Few, however, were as electrifying as the 5-foot-9, 176-pound wide receiver.

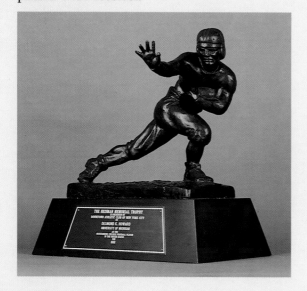

Howard was one of those rare players who drew plenty of attention whether or not he was actually part of a play. He was as dangerous as a live hand grenade. His quickness and ability to shake loose in a crowd made him an instant scoring threat even when least expected.

Howard was teamed with Elvis Grbac who also was his quarterback at Cleveland's St. Joseph High.

Howard was the first receiver in Big Ten history to lead the conference in scoring (90) as he set or tied five NCAA records and 12 single-season Michigan marks. Voted Most Valuable Player by his teammates, he set records for most points scored (138), most touchdowns (23), and most consecutive games with a scoring catch (19).

And he did it all with that magnificent smile.

"'The Catch' that won the game and propelled him to Heisman frontrunner."

THE HUMAN HIGHLIGHT FILM

For eternity, Charles Woodson's name will be linked with Tom Harmon and Desmond Howard as Michigan Men who have captured the Heisman Trophy.

Woodson's name is permanently engraved on the imposing bronze statue that symbolizes college football's finest player.

And just as permanently etched in the memories of all Michigan faithful is a kaleidoscope of magical images of dazzling, daring, and dizzying plays brought to life by Woodson in the unforgettable season of 1997.

Not only was Woodson voted the nation's finest player, he was a single-handed human highlight film. To the nation he was an endless script of gravity-defying interceptions, receptions, runs, returns, and good old-fashioned bone-jarring hits.

A sampling:

• A leaping one-handed grab of a Michigan State pass which Coach Lloyd Carr calls "the finest interception I have seen."

• A spine-snapping crunch of a Baylor receiver to signal the nation not to mess with Woodson.

• A 28-yard pass completion to quarterback Brian Griese to shock Wisconsin before the Ohio State showdown.

• A 37-yard reception to set up Michigan's first touchdown against the Buckeyes.

• An end zone leaping interception that featured Michael Jordan-like hang time to stifle Washington State in the Rose Bowl.

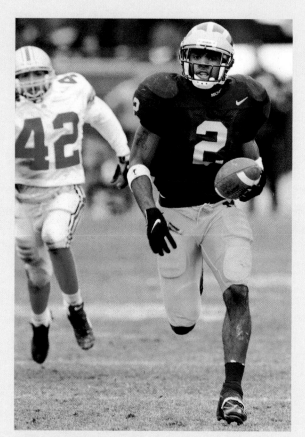

"If there was any doubt about who would win the Heisman, this punt return settled it. Just ask Ohio State."

• And his run to the Heisman — a 78-yard punt return for a touchdown to put the stake in Ohio State's heart.

Just as Michigan defied all prognosticators who laughed at the Wolverines' chances of getting through their nightmare schedule

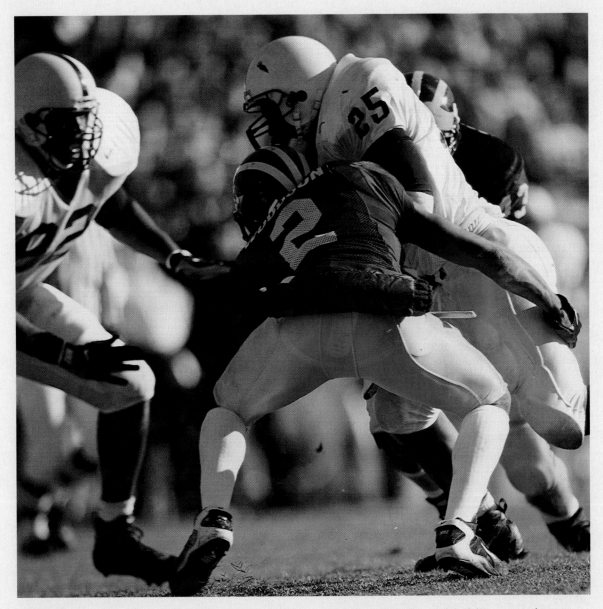

unscathed, Woodson also defied history by becoming the first primarily defensive player to win the Heisman.

And just as all the Wolverines embraced the challenge, so did Woodson.

Throughout his personal parade to history, Woodson never placed individual honors above the goals of the team. Playing unselfishly and operating within the chemistry which Coach Carr created, Woodson worked diligently and led by example.

Consequently, Michigan captured a National Championship and Woodson walked off with the most significant single honor his sport has to offer.

And Wolverine faithful were rewarded with a lifetime of memories that will forever be woven into the fabric of the Michigan Football tradition.

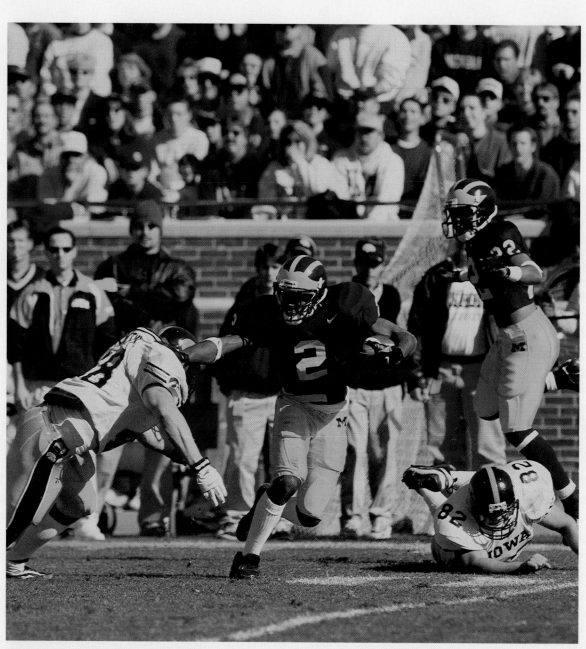

"He looks like a real-life Heisman Trophy."

"Judging by that hat, Tom Harmon looked just as good off the field as he did when he was running the ball."

"How about that 'Michigan Man' with his future wife, actress Elyse Knox?"

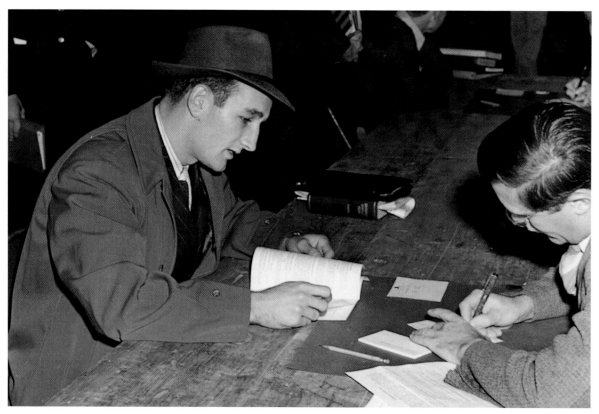

"Harmon had done it on the field. Now he was signing up to go to war."

"Here's the 1942 team signing a ball for Harmon of Michigan to carry in his plane during the war."

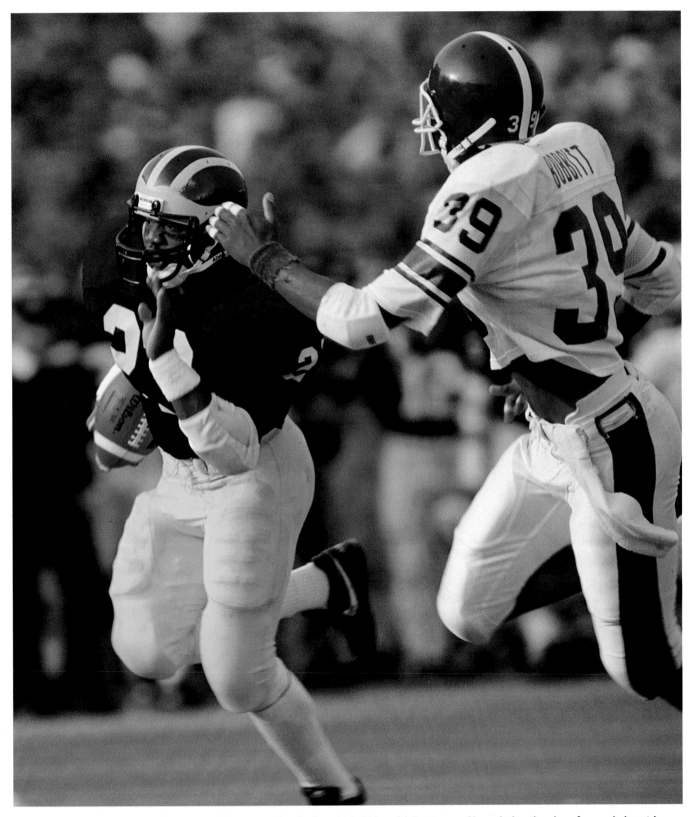

"Jamie Morris was the cutest little runner I ever saw. I only thought he'd be a kick returner. Never judge the size of a man's heart by the size of his body."

"Look at that stance. Look at that hair. That's me."

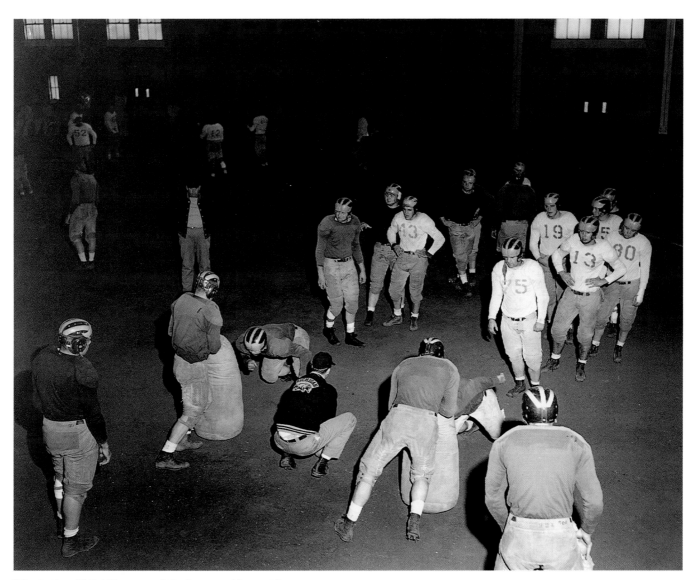

"That's the old field house and the boys working out."

"William Cunningham — Michigan's first All-American. Do you think times have changed?"

"How about those seats for a game?"

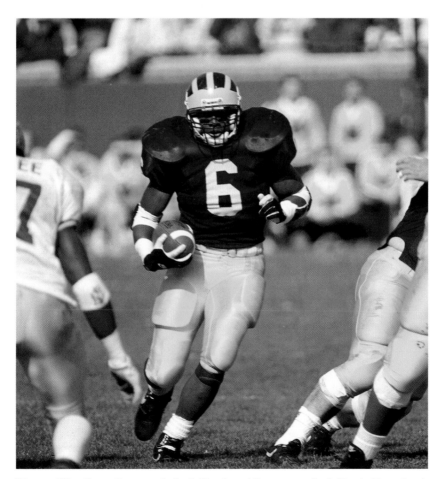

"Tyrone Wheatley — the speed of a tailback and the power of a fullback. How about 235 yards rushing in the 1993 Rose Bowl?"

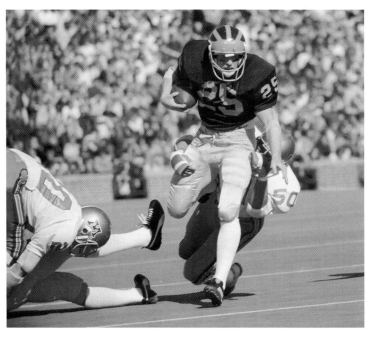

"Rob Lyttle was the most unselfish player I ever had. We moved him from tailback to fullback one year and he never said a word. He just did the job."

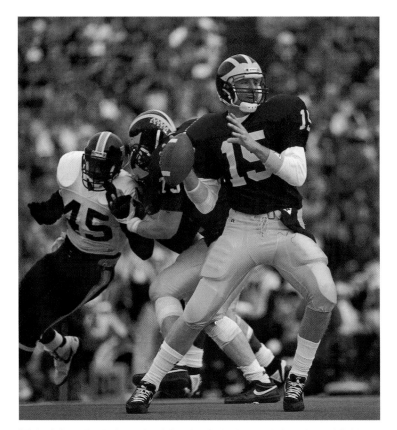

"Elvis Grbac didn't throw in high school. We had to bring him to Michigan to develop him as a passer. Check him out on Sunday afternoons now."

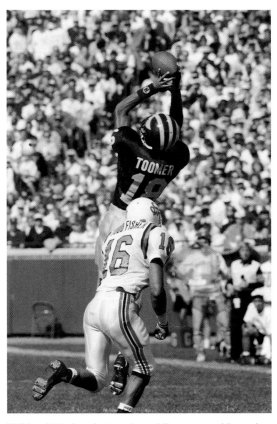

"With a little head start, Amani Toomer could touch the sky."

UFER OF MEE-SHEE-GAN

Bob Ufer was the consummate "homer" when it came to broadcasting Michigan Football. The thing that made him so special was that his passion was real. He was not a phony. He absolutely loved Michigan. And everyone loved him.

He made a three-yard Michigan run sound like a game-winning touchdown. People who listened to him on the radio while watching the game on television might not realize they were watching the same game. That's how openly he wore his love for Michigan.

Rival coaches used to tell me, "I wish we had a guy like that broadcasting our games."

On Fridays before a game, he always taped me for his pre-game show. I'll always remember the trick I played on him before our first game against Notre Dame.

"Oh boy, this is going to be a big game," he said when he walked through my door.

"Ufe, I hate to tell you this," I said.

He got real nervous.

"What's happening...what's happening?" he asked.

"Rick Leach is out," I told him.

His jaw almost hit the floor.

"No, no, no," he said.

I thought he was going to die. I had to tell him I was just kidding. That's how much he loved Michigan. He helped in recruiting. He'd do anything for the University.

He was a good man. I loved him.

"There was nothing Bob Ufer (middle right) loved more than Michigan."

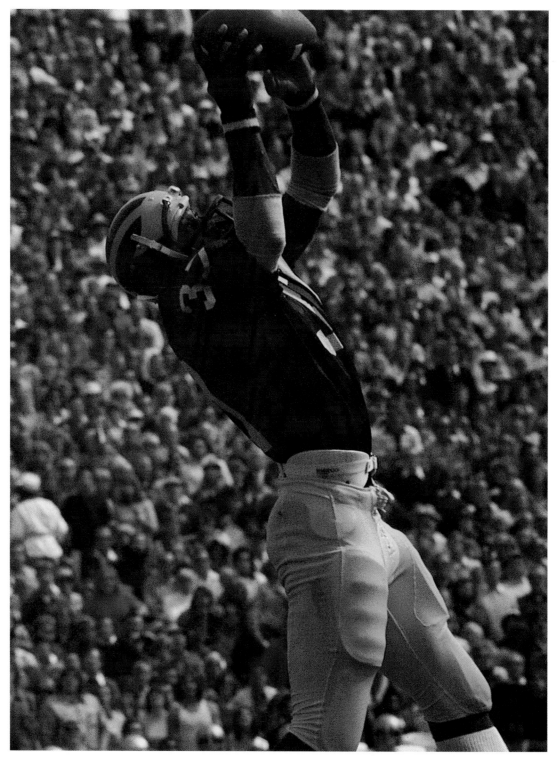

"Jim Smith was our first NFL-type receiver. He had the moves and the hands to go with them."

"Ron Johnson was quick...powerful...and I would have loved to have coached him. He finished one year before I arrived. Before he left, he set the Michigan single-game rushing record of 347 yards and scored 5 touchdowns against Wisconsin here on November 16, 1968."

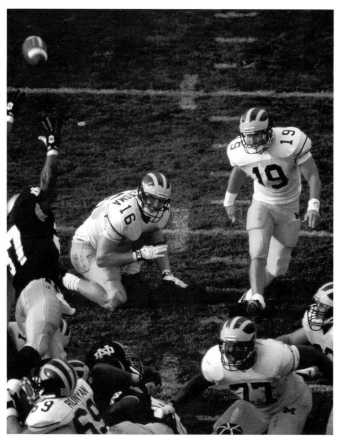

"When you kick a field goal as big as this one, you don't have to see the ball to know it's good. Remy Hamilton kicked this one with two-seconds left to beat Notre Dame, 26-24, in South Bend in 1994. That broke a lot of Irish hearts. Now isn't that too bad?"

A GIVING HERO

One incident best describes what Anthony Carter meant to his teammates and the Michigan Football tradition.

After we beat Washington in the 1981 Rose Bowl, Anthony walked into the coaches' dressing room. He had showered and dressed quickly and left the players' locker room.

"Anthony, you shouldn't be here," I said to him. "You should be over there with all the press and TV reporters."

He looked at me and said, "Coach, I've done enough of that. If I'm not there, they'll have to talk to my teammates."

That's the way Anthony Carter always was. He didn't want to stand in the locker room surrounded by all the press while his teammates, who had played their hearts out, were ignored. He was a legitimate superstar who never wanted that label.

"He wore No. 1 on his jersey. But all you had to do was look at his legs. They were skinny, but man what a big heart!"

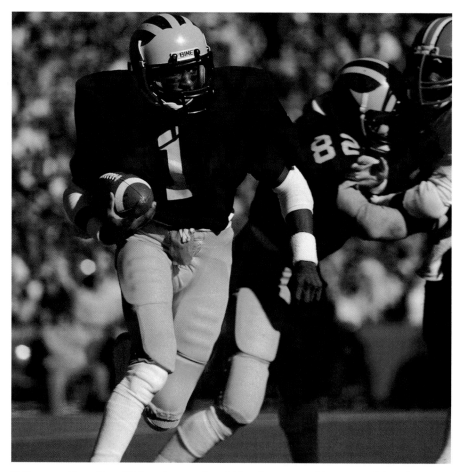

"A.C. was a three-time All-American and could break a game wide open quicker than anybody could open a bottle of pop. Number 82 is Dr. Norman Betts leading the blocking."

He had so much talent, but he was the complete team player. He was unbelievably unselfish. Everybody loved him.

The other thing that was so different about Anthony was his toughness. It was unmatched by any other receiver. He was fearless going into the middle to catch a ball. He got hit and knocked around, but he always jumped up. He was never intimidated by secondary backs coming at him.

When he first came to Michigan, we weren't exactly known as a great passing team. On the first day of practice we had our quarterbacks throwing long. It didn't matter how far they overthrew Anthony, he simply ran under the ball and caught it. None of our coaches had ever seen anything like it.

He started making the big play for us even as a freshman. The first time he returned a punt he took it in for a touchdown. Everyone expected a big play from him and he always delivered.

As a freshman in 1979 when he caught that pass with no time left and took it in for a game-winning touchdown, Indiana knew the ball was going to him. They made one mistake. They thought they'd let him catch it and then bring him down. That didn't happen to Anthony Carter with the game on the line.

THE PRIVILEGE OF MICHIGAN

To me, no coach in America asks a man to make any sacrifice.

He requests just the opposite,

Live clean, come clean, think clean,

That he stop doing all the things that destroy him physically,

Mentally, and morally,

And begin doing all the things that make him keener, finer,

And more competent.

— Fielding H. Yost

When I first came to Michigan, I brought my assistant coaches with me from Miami of Ohio.

Miami is a good university. Good educational institution. Good athletic program.

Suddenly, though, we were in the big time. As a matter of fact, there was no place bigger than the University of Michigan.

There was the tradition. There were all those great players that had made all that glorious history here. There was that beautiful big stadium.

The locker rooms, at that time, were in Yost Field House. The funny part about it was that the coaches' room was no bigger than an ordinary kitchen. We had rickety, rotten folding chairs to sit on. We hung our clothes on spikes that were nailed into two-by-fours.

One of the coaches said we had 10 times better dressing facilities back at Miami.

"Wait a minute, men," I told them.

"Did you ever sit in the same chair that Fielding H. Yost and Fritz Crisler did? No you didn't.

"Did you ever hang your clothes on the same spike as Harry Kipke and Bennie Oosterbaan did? No you didn't.

"THAT'S the difference between Michigan and every other university in the United States of America. And DON'T you forget it."

Coaching football at the University of Michigan is a very demanding position. What you always must remember, though, it is not a job.

It is a PRIVILEGE.

"That's the 1898 team with Coach Gustave Ferbert (upper right, back row)."

Since the turn of the century, there have been only 10 head football coaches at Michigan, and a couple of the early ones were only on board for a few years.

That's an awfully small number for a program more than a hundred years old. And there's a very good reason for it.

The University takes tremendous pride in placing its tradition into exactly the right hands. When a man is accepted for the position of head coach here, that is an honor. You don't see Michigan coaches politicking for any other job.

That's because all of us knew the same thing — we were privileged to hold the BEST football head coaching job anywhere in the United States of America.

Just watch how some college coaches play musical chairs. Sometimes it's the coaches who are always on the lookout to make another move. Sometimes it's the schools who make the move before a coach has a chance.

That doesn't happen at Michigan. No coach in his right mind is going to shop for flowers when he's already living smack in the middle of the most beautiful garden in the country.

There are a lot of outstanding universities all over the country. There are a number of successful football programs.

When you combine academic excellence with consistent football superiority, though, I believe there is no other school that measures up to the standards of the University of Michigan.

It's impossible to coach at Michigan without feeling the presence of all the great ones who will always remain part of the tradition.

Fielding Yost, for instance, was a man so far ahead of his time, we still haven't caught up to him today.

Can anyone imagine his vision to build a facility like Michigan Stadium way back in 1927?

"Talk about legends, that's Fielding H. Yost (right) with the great Walter Camp, University of Chicago coach, at a 1903 game. I wish I could have coached in one of those hats."

People thought he was crazy to build a stadium that would hold 72,000 people back then. And he had it constructed so that it can accommodate 130,000. He envisioned the day when Michigan Football would demand that number. And he was right.

He didn't stop with just the stadium. He built the country's first collegiate field house. He built an intramural facility to house athletics for the entire student body. And he built a golf course that ranks among the best at all universities.

Yost was a true visionary. He also was one of the most successful coaches in the history of intercollegiate football. He won 165 of 204 games. In 1901, he led Michigan to the first Rose Bowl championship and the school's first national title.

Fritz Crisler was a totally different personality than Yost. He also was brilliant and his

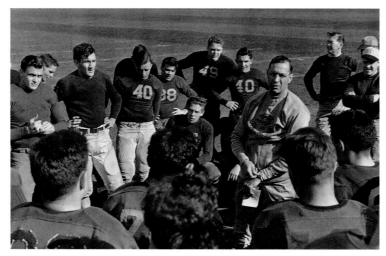

"Fritz Crisler's impromptu meetings were classics."

"You only had to tell Jim Harbaugh once."

contributions to the Michigan tradition are felt today.

Crisler was the foremost national authority on college football rules. He was the originator of two-platoon football. And in 1938, he designed the famous maize-and-blue winged helmet that still remains the most distinctive headgear in football — college or professional!

Every coach privileged to lead Michigan Football had a little different personality and brought a little different approach to the program.

But we all share a couple of qualities. Each coach had a specifically designed program. In his own way, each taught discipline. And just as important, each coach felt a sense for the tradition that the previous ones and all the players established so many years ago.

The tradition of Michigan in academics and football is a powerful recruiting tool. There are other great academic institutions. There are other outstanding football programs.

But no other school in America combines the two as well as Michigan. The University and its tradition is the greatest recruiting weapon any coach could ask for.

In order to be successful in coaching over a long period of time, you had better enjoy

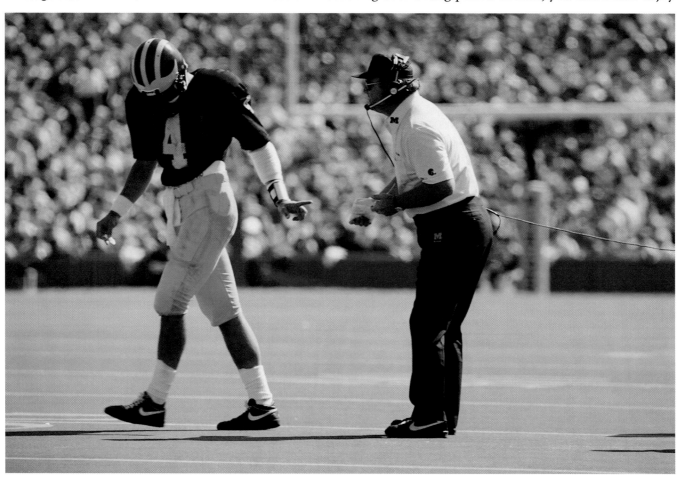

young people. You better enjoy teaching them both on and off the field.

There's pressure to win at any Division-I football program. In fact, I believe there is more pressure now than at any time in our history.

The great coaches, though, create their own special kind of pressure. It's the pressure they feel for making sure all those young players walk away from the program as men once their playing career is finished.

If a coach can help to properly shape the character of those young men to last a lifetime, then that coach was successful regardless what the won-lost record reads.

Every one of those men who coached at Michigan left a lasting impression on each young life he touched. Each coach did so because the Michigan Football program has been founded on honesty and integrity since the first time a ball was kicked.

When I look back during my tenure here, I know there were times when we might have won a couple more games or finished higher in the rankings by picking up a certain player. The price, though, was breaking the rules.

That was NOT going to happen at Michigan. It never happened then and it will not happen now.

Fielding Yost could not have explained the essence of coaching any better than when he said "No coach in America asks a man to make any sacrifice...He requests just the opposite...Live clean, come clean, think clean."

That says it all.

THAT'S the long string that continues to run through all the football coaches at the University of Michigan.

"Youth clinics were always fun, and who could imagine who might be the next Michigan star."

THE ARCHITECT OF TRADITION

FIELDING H. YOST
1901-1923, 1925-1926
(165-29-10)

"Yost was a hands-on coach. He liked to lead by example. Look at him move that ball."

Fielding H. Yost was a visionary long before he put his law degree on the shelf to become, arguably, the architect of big-time college football.

Prior to realizing his dream of making the University of Michigan the premier athletic complex in the country, though, he was an equally magnificent football coach.

For his time, there was none better.

"He was a great coach," Bo said. "It's hard to say what the competition was like back then, but he was the best of whatever it was."

That's as understated as Bo saying he "sort of" enjoys a Michigan victory over Ohio State.

Yost was a professor of football who believed the game taught character. It showed young men how to live properly. He did not believe in drinking, smoking, or carousing. He taught his players that abstinence from such practices is not a sacrifice, but rather the proper way to live.

"He always taught by example," recalled Kip Taylor. The ninety-year-old retiree who still resides in Ann Arbor scored the first touchdown in Michigan Stadium in 1927. He was a freshman and practiced under Yost during the legend's last coaching season in 1926.

"He'd do little things to make sure everyone was prepared," Taylor said. "One day he took all the ends to the goal line and stepped

"Willie Heston — one of Fielding Yost's first recruits in 1904 turned out to be one of Michigan's greats."

"Look at those eyes on Germany Schulz. Try staring at those from across the line."

From 1901-1923, and again in 1925-1926, Yost-led Michigan teams set the standards for major college football.

From 1901-1905, Michigan played 56 consecutive games without a loss. That string included winning streaks of 29 and 26 games. In those five seasons, Michigan outscored its opponents, 2,821 to 42.

"The numbers were awesome," Bo said. "But he was a defensive coach. That's what made him so great. All great coaches are defensive coaches."

Yost finished with a 165-29-10 record and won 10 Big Ten titles in a span of 15 years. He also led Michigan to a 49-0 rout over Stanford in the first Rose Bowl in 1901.

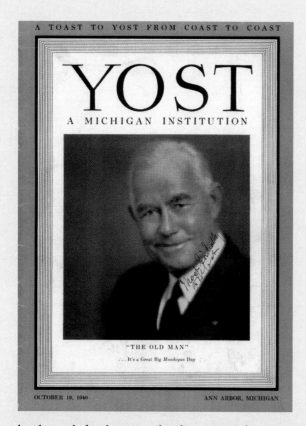

A TOAST TO YOST FROM COAST TO COAST

YOST

A MICHIGAN INSTITUTION

"THE OLD MAN"

...It's a Great Big Meecheegan Day

OCTOBER 19, 1940   ANN ARBOR, MICHIGAN

back and forth over the line several times. Then he looked at us and said, 'You can run over this line a hundred times and it doesn't mean a thing if you don't have that little brown thing in your hands.' It was details...details...details with Mr. Yost."

Yost used the forward pass in 1910 — two years ahead of Knute Rockne, who is generally credited with its inception. In addition, Yost created the position of linebacker with one of his prize pupils — All-American Germany Schulz.

More than anything, Yost taught preparedness as if it were a religion.

"Many have the will to win, but few have the will to prepare," was one of his credos.

So zealous was Yost about preparation that he often put on pads to demonstrate proper blocking and tackling techniques.

Yost transcended his role of coach and visionary who built the Michigan Stadium,

Yost Field House, the Michigan Golf Course and the Intramural Building.

He also was a genuinely romantic, almost make-believe, character who commanded his share of the national sporting spotlight in the era of such giants as Babe Ruth. In fact, legendary writer Ring Lardner once said that Yost actually possessed more personality than Ruth.

And Yost wasn't afraid to talk about himself in a fashion where everybody listened. He loved to talk. And he was always prepared to expound on his beloved "Meeshegan."

"He'd talk to anybody," Taylor said. "He'd walk up-and-down State Street and talk football to anybody who'd listen. There'd be tobacco juice dripping down his cheek and his hat would be half off his head, but he'd talk about the game. He loved football. And he loved Michigan."

Howard Wikel, who played from 1943-47, was a boy in his father's pharmacy on University when Yost regularly visited.

"Mr. Yost would come into the store and sit at a little table near the door," Wikel recalls. "As students came in, he'd grab them by the arm. He'd say, 'Sit down here me boy...I want to explain something to you.'"

Yost then would diagram plays using knives

"Let me tell you about Howard Wikel. If you want to know anything about Michigan Football, Ann Arbor or just about anything, you better ask Howard."

"Mr. Yost looked like the big-time executive in his new office."

and forks and salt and pepper shakers as imaginary players.

"Then he'd give lessons on the Civil War," Wikel said. "He was a very scholarly person on the war."

Yost spoke with a touch of West Virginia accent and used it to his advantage while spinning his yarns.

"He spoke in stories," Taylor said. "He illustrated everything he talked about with a story. And everybody loved it."

Even in his advancing years, everyone but his closest friends referred to him as Coach or Mr. Yost.

"You had to really know him to call him by his first name," Taylor said. "Even though he was as down-to-earth as a bushel of apples, people just naturally spoke to him with great respect."

Almost a century after first arriving in Ann Arbor, Yost still enjoys the respect accorded a legitimate legend.

He was a first and only. He remains the revered Mr. Yost.

A CRAFTSMAN KNOWN AS CRISLER

HERBERT O. (FRITZ) CRISLER

1938-1947
(71-16-3)

Images of Fritz Crisler range from majestic to aloof.

"There was a majesty about him," said Howard Wikel, who was a reserve halfback on his teams. "There was a certain charm. He could have been an actor, a doctor, or anything he would have wanted to be."

After graduating from the University of Chicago with a degree in psychology, Crisler decided against medical school to pursue a career in coaching.

"At the University of Chicago, Fritz Crisler was quite a player himself."

"He didn't allow people to get too close to him," said Don Lund, one of Michigan's finest all-around athletes who played fullback for Crisler. "Yet after each game, he'd go around to all the players and put his arm around them. If we lost, he'd encourage us to 'get 'em next week.'"

Crisler was unforgivably meticulous. He never allowed coincidence to carve his destiny. He was the master of design and carefully sculpted everything within his influence.

"Fritz took that 1947 National Champion team to the Rose Bowl and proceeded to hammer USC, 49-0."

"I don't care how well you knew him," Wikel said. "You didn't say hello to him until he said something first. That's just the way it was."

While some regarded Crisler's personality as being somewhat aloof, he was consumed by the smallest detail in his pursuit of Michigan excellence.

His legacy to the Michigan Football tradition transcends his 10-year record of 71-16-3.

It was Crisler in his first year who introduced the famous winged helmets in 1938. Until then, Michigan's helmets were black. Crisler sought distinction. He also felt the design would help facilitate his single-wing offense that demanded speed and deception.

It was Crisler who introduced the two-platoon system when Michigan played top-ranked Army on October 12, 1945 in Yankee Stadium. The inception revolutionized college football.

It also was Crisler who led Michigan back into national football prominence. During his tenure as coach, Michigan finished lower than second in conference play only twice.

Crisler capped his coaching career by directing Michigan to a 49-0 rout of Southern California in the 1948 Rose Bowl to finish an unbeaten season as the national champion.

It was that team that nicknamed Crisler "The Lord."

No disrespect was intended. In fact, it was done out of respect for the way Crisler was always thoroughly prepared and seemed never to overlook even the most minute detail.

"He was always in control," said Bump Elliott who played halfback on that national championship team and later coached at Michigan. "He was uncompromising, but always with good reason. He didn't demand respect, he earned it."

Crisler's preparation was as thorough as the most complex mathematical equation. Each move was orchestrated. Even for

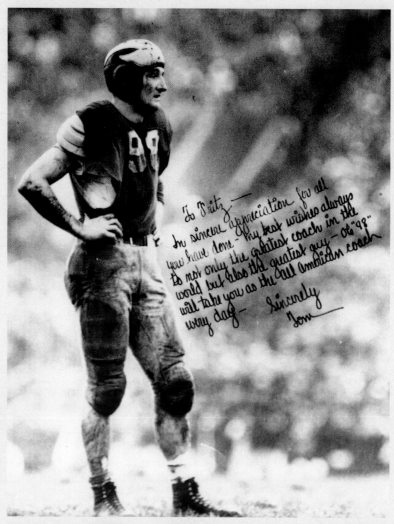

To Fritz —
In sincere appreciation for all you have done — my best wishes always to not only the greatest coach in the world but also the greatest guy — of "98" will take you as the All American coach every day — Sincerely, Tom

"The note from Harmon sort of sums up the way all of Crisler's players felt. He was a coach...a teacher...a leader...a man."

practices, he used handwritten notes in red and blue pencil.

His pregame and halftime speeches to his teams were delivered with theatrical flair.

"He had a unique commanding personality that gained the absolute attention and respect of those in his presence," said Pete Elliott, who played on that 1947 team and also the 1948 national champion team.

"We would wait for and listen to his every word even to the point of his pauses being dramatic and meaningful."

In his own singular style, Crisler had the ability to motivate like a Sunday morning TV preacher. He never raised his voice. He never cursed. He was clinically articulate. His eyes were like lasers and communicated as well as his words.

"He got the nickname 'Gimlet Eye' from the way that his stare could affect anyone

"That single wing play, 22-power, could take the ball off the flank with double teams inside and outside."

who was the recipient of the stare," said Tom Kuzma who played two years for him.

There was the celebrated incident when All-American halfback Bob Chappuis injured his hamstring while practicing for the 1948 Rose Bowl. While Chappuis laid on the ground, Crisler calmly looked down.

"Good thing it didn't happen to someone who could run," Crisler said with cold deliberation.

Crisler, of course, was concerned for his star. It was merely his way of motivating Chappuis along with showing his team that it could survive adversity.

"I don't know about the rest of the guys, but I felt a lot better after he said that," said Bruce Hilkene who captained that team. "He wanted to show everyone that this was a team effort."

Chappuis also understood what Crisler was doing. And Chappuis responded exactly as his coach hoped he would. He threw for 188 yards and two touchdowns. He also carried the ball 13 times for 91 yards.

Norma Bentley was Crisler's longtime secretary. In the early '90s, Chappuis visited her in an Ann Arbor nursing home. It wasn't until then that he discovered how concerned Crisler had been.

"She told me that Coach Crisler really was worried I wouldn't be able to play in that Rose Bowl," Chappuis said. "That did make me feel good."

Crisler's gift for motivation was unchallenged.

"His pregame pep talks were fabulous," said Al Wistert. "Before the Michigan State game one year he said, 'Nobody ever heard of Michigan State before they beat us. You made them. Now I want you to go out there and break them!'

"Against Minnesota one year he said, 'This game will take all you've got — 60-minutes of unrelenting everlasting pressure — 60-minutes of sacrifice and a lifetime to remember.'"

Wistert also remembers how Crisler was relentless in reminding his men to play and live properly:

"Often he reminded us — 'Remember you are Michigan men. You represent a great university. Don't ever do anything on or off the field of play which might tarnish this revered name — the University of Michigan.'"

For reasons only Crisler knew for sure, however, Crisler preferred to keep his distance. Not only from his players, but also from all but a handful of his closest friends.

After his coaching career, Crisler remained as Athletic Director until his retirement in 1968. Because of his unmatched knowledge of rules and his discipline for details, he was regarded as one of the nation's most influential administrators.

Although reluctantly, even the legendary Woody Hayes acknowledged Crisler's stature. Bo served as an assistant to Hayes at the time.

"It got to Woody," Bo said. "He used to say 'Crisler runs the whole damn conference...A damn guy from Michigan...But he's one smart son of a gun.'"

Crisler was an enigma. But he also left footprints on the Michigan tradition that will remain a century from now.

A TEAM FOR THE AGES

They were called the "Mad Magicians." Who knows for sure if they had the most pure talent? Everyone knows for certain, though, that no other college football team in the country performed at a higher level.

At the time, they were so young. Now...several of them are gone.

Some had served their country in World War II. Others would be called to fight in the Korean War only a few years later.

The glories of that team have withstood the test of time. More than a half-century has passed since that 1947 Michigan team went undefeated, including a 49-0 Rose Bowl rout over the University of Southern California to finish as national champion.

Lunar landings, a presidential assassination, an even deadlier Asian war,

"Bob Chappuis was big-time. Michigan belongs on the cover of *Time*."

"Here's the backfield: (left to right) Bump Elliott, Howard Yerges, Jack Weisenberger, and Bob Chappuis."

"Now that's styling...Bump Elliott and Bob Chappuis with Hollywood star Marlene Dietrich at the 1948 Rose Bowl."

and a technological revolution all have followed that little precious sliver of time that once seemed as though it would never end.

It was the final coaching season for the legendary Fritz Crisler. Like a veteran Broadway performer, he sensed it was the perfect time for his final performance.

The closeness of that team bonded teammates for life. So much so that every five years all remaining members gather for a reunion. Ann Arbor hosted the first nine. For their 50th anniversary, team members planned something special. In 1992, they decided to

meet in Pasadena at the 1998 Rose Bowl.

"What a miraculous turn of events for the 1997 team to be in the same situation as we were," said All-American halfback Bob Chappuis.

Just as its predecessor from a half-century ago, the 1997 team capped off an undefeated season with a victory in the Rose Bowl to finish as national champion.

"There are so many wonderful memories," Chappuis said. "But the Rose Bowl victory probably symbolizes everything.

"The whole picture doesn't really hit you

"Look at that 1947 squad. You can't run the kind of offense they did without tremendous discipline and deception."

until years later. There aren't too many people in the world who can sit around in their pajamas and robe at night and say that they played for an undefeated team that won the Rose Bowl and finished as the national champion. It takes time to really appreciate all of that. Those young men of 1997 don't even know yet just how much they accomplished."

Certainly that 1947 squad had talent. Chappuis and Bump Elliott earned All-American honors. They had plenty of support from players like Bob Mann, Bruce Hilkene, Dominic Tomasi, J.T. White, Stu Wilkins, Bill Pritula, Dick Rifenburg, Howard Yerges, and Jack Wiesenburger, among others.

All admit, though, there may have been more talented teams.

"We didn't have the greatest players," Chappuis said. "But Coach Crisler was able to get us to put it altogether and always perform as a team. He always stressed one thing — you had to play better than you know how. Push the other team in the direction you want it to go and don't give up."

That 1947 squad was a perfect reflection of the discipline Crisler always practiced and preached.

"He asked each player to dedicate his efforts to playing football each day one percent better than the previous day," Chappuis said. "He said, 'if you will collectively do this, I will guarantee you now that you will be part of a winning football program.'"

Chappuis calls Crisler "The epitome of dignity."

And that's the way his teams always performed.

While his health permitted, Crisler regularly

june 4, 1973

There are times when the heart is too full for utterance and being with you on your 25th reunion, for me, was one of those times. Even had I been gifted or adequately endowed to express my true feelings any effort would have fallen far short. My human speech would have been naught, my human testimony inadequate, my human estimates futile. Only my silent thoughts fruitful, my silent meditations sacred.

As we travel down the weary path of life thru the garden of our memories no doubt the echoes of yesteryears cheers will become dim, the winners wreaths may wither, the blue in our victory ribbons may fade, trophies may become tarnished, the gleam of our medals lose luster, but the emotional experiences of joy and elation, heartaches and disappointments can never be shared by others. Robust friendships were created. none was lukewarm but all very alive and everlastingly vivid.

These friendships, thru sunshine and shadows, will stand forever as a brilliant beacon high in the halls of our memories framed in majestic reverence.

May good fortune always smile on you and yours, all ways.

Your Old Coach with abiding affection

"Fritz loved all his boys. But that 1947 squad was special. He taught them always to stick together. Isn't this some kind of letter for their 25th reunion?"

attended the five-year reunions of that 1947 squad. Shortly after the 25th reunion in 1973, each member of the team received a letter from their coach expressing his feelings for "his boys" which he rarely displayed.

"I framed it and have it hanging on a wall in my house," Chappuis said. "Sometimes I look at it and it still brings tears to my eyes."

THE LEADERS OF MEN

In spite of being more than a century old, only a handful of men have been chosen to lead the storied Michigan Football program.

MIKE MURPHY and FRANK CRAWFORD
(1891, 4-5-0 record) were the first official coaches. Prior to their appointment, the Michigan football program operated for 11 seasons without a coach.

Crawford initiated Michigan's first advance schedule.

FRANK E. BARBOUR
(1892-1893, 14-8-0) led Michigan on a then-ambitious 12 and 10 game schedule. In 8 of his 14 victories, Michigan posted shutouts.

WILLIAM L. McCAULEY
(1894-1895, 17-2-1) was a Princeton graduate and Michigan medical school student when he was named coach. Michigan's 12-4 victory over Cornell in 1894 marked the first time in collegiate football history that a western school defeated an established power from the east.

WILLIAM D. WARD
(1896, 9-1) also was a Princeton graduate. His team allowed only 11 points all season.

GUSTAVE H. FERBERT
(1897-1899, 24-3-1) became coach after the student-alumni advisory board determined only former Michigan students could coach football. An 1897 graduate, Ferbert led Michigan to its first Big Ten title in 1898.

LANGDON (BIFF) LEA
(1900, 7-2-1) was a Princeton graduate and took over after the former students-only rule had been rescinded. A strict disciplinarian, Lea posted a rule on the wall of the gymnasium stating the word "can't" is not in the football vocabulary.

FIELDING H. YOST
(1901-1923, 1925-1926, 165-29-10) remains the first among Michigan coaching legends. Known as the "Point-a-Minute" teams, Yost-led squads played 56 straight games without a loss from 1901-1905. In those five years, the Wolverines outscored their opponents 2,821 to 42.

The 1901 team went 10-0 and won the Big Ten title before routing Stanford, 49-0, in the first Rose Bowl. Michigan won the national championship in 1901, 1902, 1903, and 1904. Under Yost, Michigan won 10 Big Ten titles and 20 of his players were named All-American.

Yost served as Director of Athletics from 1921-1941. Under Yost's vision, the University built Michigan Stadium, an 18-hole Alister MacKenzie-designed golf course, the nation's first intramural sports building, and the nation's first multi-purpose field house now known as the Yost Ice Arena.

GEORGE LITTLE
(1924, 6-2-0) was a defensive-minded coach and his team shut out opponents in five of its six victories. He had served as Yost's top assistant for two years and left Michigan to become Athletic Director at the University of Wisconsin.

ELTON E. (TAD) WIEMAN
(1927-1928, 9-6-1) was a three-season star for the Wolverines at tackle and fullback, where he earned all-conference honors. Wieman also earned Phi Beta Kappa honors for his classroom achievements.

HARRY G. KIPKE

(1929-1937, 46-26-4) was Michigan's first nine-letterman from football, basketball, and baseball. He was one of the nation's greatest kickers and was named an All-American halfback.

From 1930 through 1933, Michigan won four straight Big Ten titles and was named national champion in 1932 and 1933. Kipke, Yost, and Bo are the only coaches to have led Michigan to four consecutive conference championships.

HERBERT O. (FRITZ) CRISLER

(1938-1947, 71-16-3) led consistently disciplined and superior teams. Only twice during his ten-year career did Michigan finish lower than second in the conference.

Crisler was an offensive-minded coach whose innovations piled up yards. His .805 winning percentage ranks him second in school history behind Yost (minimum 50 games). Before turning his full-time attention to his position of Athletic Director, Crisler's last game was a 49-0 rout of Southern California in the 1948 Rose Bowl to clinch the national title.

BENNIE G. OOSTERBAAN

(1948-1958, 63-33-4) became Michigan's first three-time All-American football player. He won three letters in football, basketball, and baseball.

Following his graduation in 1928, he turned down contracts from professional baseball and football organizations in order to join the Michigan coaching staff. He had a brilliant mind for offense and coached backs and ends for Crisler.

In 1948, he guided the Wolverines to a 9-0 record and a national championship.

CHALMERS W. (BUMP) ELLIOTT

(1959-1968, 51-42-2) holds the rare distinction of both coaching and playing for Michigan teams that won a Big Ten championship and a Rose Bowl.

In 1964, he directed Michigan to a 9-1 record and a 34-7 victory over Oregon State in the Rose Bowl. As an All-American on the Wolverines' national championship team of 1947, he was called the greatest right halfback Crisler had ever seen.

Under Elliott, Michigan produced five All-Americans.

GLENN E. (BO) SCHEMBECHLER

(1969-1989, 194-48-5) has more wins than any other coach in Michigan history. His teams won or tied 13 Big Ten titles. He guided 17 Michigan teams to bowl games, including 10 Rose Bowls. Under Bo, 17 Michigan teams finished in the wire services' Top Ten. In addition to his coaching duties, Bo served as Athletic Director from 1988-1990.

GARY O. MOELLER

(1990-1994, 44-13-3) guided Michigan to four bowl victories in five years, including the 1993 Rose Bowl. Under Moeller, Michigan won three Big Ten championships and had five finishes in the nation's top 20. Michigan also set a Big Ten record by winning 19 straight conference games between 1990-1992.

LLOYD CARR

(1995-present) has delivered more than a national championship to the University of Michigan. He has provided the promise of continuing football excellence through traditional Michigan trademarks — commitment...integrity...and team unity. His unselfish program perfectly reflects the foundation upon which the Michigan tradition is based.

In three years under Carr, the Wolverines have posted a 29-8 record. In 1997, Michigan set a school record with a 12-0 mark and its first national championship since 1948.

Carr has been part of the Michigan program since 1980, when he started as an assistant under Bo. He was named Interim Head Coach before the start of the 1995 season and was made the 17th permanent Head Coach on November 13 of that year.

For his efforts in 1997, Carr was named National Coach of the Year. Based upon his tireless work ethic and commitment to the University, that award may find its way to Ann Arbor again in the future.

THE ELLIOTT LEGACY

No one captures the essence of Bump Elliott better than Jim Conley.

"He was born to be on a Wheaties box," said the 1964 Michigan captain whose team went on to crush Oregon State, 34-7, in the 1965 Rose Bowl under Coach Elliott.

With his Huck Finn looks and Will Rogers personality, Elliott could charm Ebenezer Scrooge into playing Santa Claus.

"Can you imagine any parent of a prospective recruit not wanting to entrust their boy to Bump when he went off to college?" asks Don Lund, another former Michigan standout.

More importantly, Elliott backed up that All-American image with an All-American playing career before taking over the reigns at his alma mater.

Under Fritz Crisler, Elliott helped to lead

"That's Bump and Pete. If they aren't the picture of the All-American boys then you don't like apple pie."

Michigan to the first of back-to-back national championships in 1947. Elliott played right halfback and Bob Chappuis was at left. Both were named All-Americans.

During that season, just two years after returning from overseas duty with the Marines, Elliott led the conference in scoring with 54 points. He also was named Most Valuable Player in the conference.

"He was the greatest right halfback I have ever seen," Crisler once said.

One of Elliott's teammates was his brother, Pete. Both were two-way standouts and comprise one of the most celebrated names in Michigan history.

After serving as an assistant in 1957 and 1958 under Bennie Oosterbaan, Elliott took over as head coach for the 1959 season. He guided the Wolverines to the Rose Bowl victory in 1965.

"There was nothing you could dislike about Bump," Conley said. "He was a great teacher and leader. More importantly, he was a straight shooter. He was so honest."

After that Rose Bowl victory, the Wolverines scuffled for the next three seasons.

"Bump was a terrific coach," Conley said. "Sometimes people don't realize how tough it is to follow a couple of legends like Crisler and Oosterbaan."

Before leaving, however, Elliott assembled a championship team in-waiting. His 1968 team finished the year with an 8-2 record and was ready for Bo to ride them to a Big Ten championship and another Rose Bowl appearance the next season.

"I always joke with Bo that we helped to set

"Going from player to coach at Michigan had to be some kind of special feeling for Bump."

the table for him," Conley cracked. "But I think he had a pretty good idea of what he could do."

During his coaching career, Elliott faced brother Pete, who had taken over the head position at Illinois.

The Elliott name will forever live as a major part of the Michigan tradition.

FOREVER BLUE

For Bennie Oosterbaan, there was no better place on earth than the University of Michigan.

It had always been his little piece of paradise from the time he was one of the school's most gifted all-around athletes until he died following a distinguished coaching career.

Perhaps no one cherished the Michigan spirit as much as Oosterbaan. His gift for eternity was provided by his protégé who was as equally athletically gifted and whose love for the University remains unchallenged.

"It was Bennie's wish to always be part of the University," explained former All-American Ron Kramer whose No. 87 was retired by Oosterbaan.

"Before he died we discussed every detail. We did everything with dignity and with the intention of allowing a great man to enjoy his reward for eternity."

Kramer tenderly placed Oosterbaan's ashes in all the places his old coach held dearest to his heart. He placed some near the stadium tunnel and all around the field where Oosterbaan played as a three-time All-American end. He placed some around Yost Field House where he starred on the basketball court. And he placed some around the baseball diamond where Oosterbaan also was a standout.

Oosterbaan had several opportunities to play sports professionally. Instead, he decided never to leave Michigan. Nothing gave him greater happiness than coaching for his life's passion.

"Bennie was Michigan," Kramer said. "He always will be. For him there was nothing

"Maybe the greatest athlete in Michigan history."

"Sometimes the natives get a little restless."

"Nice car, but Bennie never took it too far out of Ann Arbor. That was home and he loved it."

greater in life than wearing the Michigan uniform or leading young men to Michigan glory."

Oosterbaan had the ability to make everyone feel he was the neighbor next door. He was a players' coach. He had an ability to make everyone feel at ease. His players called him "Bennie" or "Coach." He was never a shouter, but his message was always clear.

"He had that look," said Kramer who was a two-time All-American under Oosterbaan. "He looked at everyone but he gave you the feeling he was looking squarely at you."

His theme never wavered.

"He spoke of the Michigan tradition," Kramer said. "He spoke of pride. He always said that everyone at Michigan is family. Not just the team he was coaching but everyone who had played before us. They were all looking at us and were actually part of us. He was extremely sincere because he loved Michigan that much."

Oosterbaan became the first assistant under Fritz Crisler and took over the head job in 1948. Oosterbaan was a genius on offense and is credited with masterminding the plays for the celebrated "Mad Magicians."

In his first season, Oosterbaan guided Michigan to a 9-0 record and a national championship. For his efforts he was named National Coach of the Year.

As a player, Oosterbaan had few peers. As

an end, he became the first of only two Michigan players to win All-American honors three times (1925-1927). His number 47 was retired.

He was named All-American twice in basketball. He was an All-Big Ten baseball player and finished his career with nine varsity letters. He refused professional baseball and football offers to remain as a coach at his beloved Michigan.

"There was nothing phony about Bennie," Kramer said. "He believed in Michigan and wasn't afraid to say so. He believed very strongly that all of us are Michigan. And we must live up to the standards that are expected of us."

"From his helicopter, Bennie Oosterbaan had a pretty good view of spring practice."

"Friedman was the 'other' Benny and he was pretty good. He was the guy throwing all those passes to Oosterbaan."

PATIENCE...PERSISTENCE... PERFECTION

The skeptics have scattered. Even they know the future of the Michigan Football tradition is safe.

Under Lloyd Carr, it's more secure than under Lloyds of London.

There was the 1997 national championship. There was the Rose Bowl victory. There was Michigan's first-ever 12-win season. There was the Coach of the Year Award for Carr.

That warm glow of security, however, transcends all the numbers.

"That 1997 team didn't just happen overnight," Bo said. "Lloyd finally got the chance to put together his own program. He put together his own coaching staff and his own brand of recruits. Everyone is committed to the team and to the University of Michigan."

What Bo can't say is that Carr, in his own way, has resurrected the formula that Bo himself molded so magnificently for 21 seasons of Michigan's most glorious history.

Trying to imitate the character of Bo is impossible. He's a precious colorful chip of history that comes around only once in every lifetime. In the last 100 years, the University of Michigan has been blessed by two. At the turn of the century there was Fielding H. Yost.

Carr is more like everybody's favorite uncle. In a quiet unbending manner, he's the guy with the strong shoulder. He's always there when needed most.

Despite the personality disparity between Carr and Bo, both are strikingly similar in

"His 1997 National Championship team reflected the best coaching job I have seen since I've been at the University of Michigan."

their commitment to Michigan. Above all else, both believe in doing things honestly and the right way.

"All you have to do is look at the type of kids Lloyd goes after," Bo said. "They're all fine athletes. But they all have character. None are bigger than the team. Individual players don't win games...Michigan does."

Like all his predecessors, Carr is a tireless worker. During the recruiting season, no head coach in the country works the phones and pounds the pavement any more doggedly than Carr.

"I've watched him over the years," Bo said. "That's one of the reasons I hired him in the first place. If he really wants a kid, he doesn't

"Not just the Rose Bowl champions...the National Champions!"

stop. And you can be sure that kid has as much character as he does talent."

Bo hired Carr for the 1980 season as the defensive secondary coach. Bo liked more than Carr's football savvy.

"I knew one thing for sure if I brought Lloyd Carr on to my staff," Bo said. "I knew I'd never have to worry about him. He's a quality character. He's a man.

"He's tremendously gifted in motivation. He's emotional. He can't hide how he feels. He's honest. The guys believe in him. He communicates with all the kids and always tells them the truth. He's good for Michigan because he represents everything the university stands for. Now just watch how well he does because the 1997 season did for his program exactly what that 1969 win over Ohio State did for mine."

Carr certainly appreciates all the accolades that go along with a season like the Wolverines enjoyed in 1997. But he savors what the team has meant to the tradition

more than all the individual honors.

"The 1997 team has left a legacy to every Michigan team that follows," he said. "Every person who was part of it and every Michigan fan can stand very tall. It was a team that met every challenge. It was an unselfish team that accomplished all of its goals together. It was a team that simply refused to quit. It was a true Michigan team in every sense of the word."

Carr was a three-sport star and an all-state quarterback at Riverview High School. He played three seasons for Missouri and was the backup quarterback on the Tigers' 1966 Sugar Bowl championship team. For his senior year, he transferred to Northern Michigan University and quarterbacked the Wildcats to an undefeated season.

"I'm the luckiest college coach in the country," Carr says modestly with that same boyish grin he flashed at Riverview High. "I've got the best job in America. Where else would anyone want to be except at Michigan?"

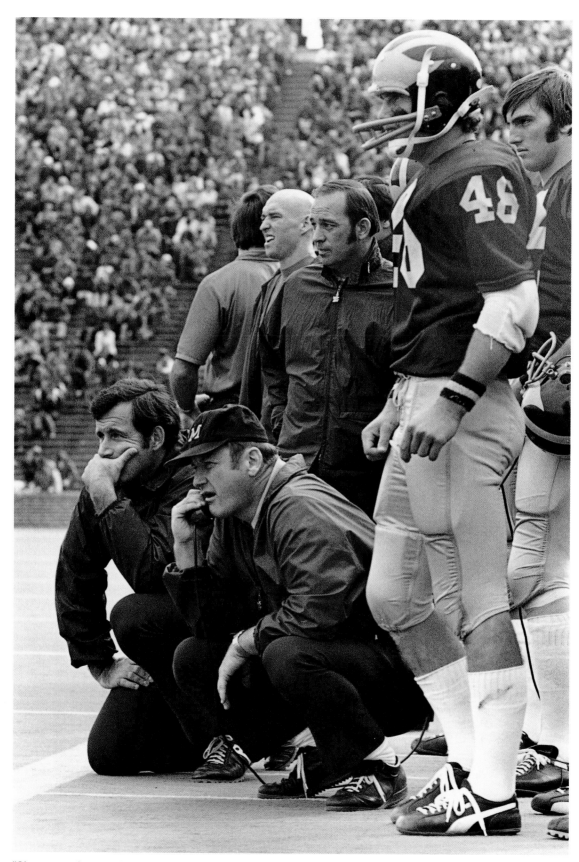

"Give me a minute and I'll think of something."

"Gary Moeller was a tremendously innovative offensive coach and as hard working a coach as I've seen."

FROM MY OWN PLAY BOOK

The 54-55 Draw was one of the favorite plays I kept in my play book.

Except for short yardage or goal line downs, I called this play on any down anywhere on the field. The beauty of this play was that you could pass or run the draw off the same formation. The draw play looked like a play action pass because the protection looked nearly the same. It was hard for the defense to distinguish whether their linebackers should be dropping back to defend the pass or step up to stop the draw.

We showed the play early in the game to set up the defense. We ran it on first, second or third down.

And it was very effective.

<u>54-55 DRAW</u>

129

COACHING POINTS:	1) Good splits 2) Release and block of TE 3) Timing and read of TB and BSG 4) Seal of BS.
CALLS:	4

BLOCKING RULES:

FSWR:	Run crack course and block inside deep defender.
FSTE:	Release inside for FS-BSLB.
FST:	Zoom block down lineman on, inside.
FSG:	Odd: drive inside. Even: fold unless tackle covered, then take #1.
C:	Odd: backside lead #0 to EOL. Even: block BS #1.
BSG:	Set and then pull to block first LB FS. (Even: MLB eagle: FSLB).
BST:	Set and take BS #2.
BSE:	Release inside for BS LB.
BSWR:	Crossfield and block middle 1/3.
FB:	Block the call.
TB:	Ball.
QB:	Give ball to TB. Fake 54-55 pass.

"It was a privilege for me just standing with these men (left to right) Harry Kipke, Fritz Crisler, Bennie Oosterbaan, Bump Elliot, and myself."

"That's the coach talking and everybody better listen."

"These guys go all the way back to 1940. Any coach would take this backfield today. That's (from the left) Forest Evashevski, Norm Call, Bob Westfall and the great Tom Harmon. Beautiful!"

"That's Fielding H. Yost and his team on a trolley ride at the 1902 Rose Bowl. Incidentally, in the game, Michigan nipped Stanford, 49-0."

"Does anybody recognize the crafty left-hander? Here comes the heat."

"A coach in the making. That's Harry Kipke punting a ball for Coach Yost. How about that form?"

"January 1, 1981 — my first Rose Bowl victory. We closed out the season with 22 consecutive quarters without allowing a touchdown against us. When we finished, we were the best team in the nation."

BETTER THAN THE HATFIELDS & M^cCOYS

Woody...you're warming up on the wrong side of the field.

— Bo Schembechler

There is NO greater rivalry in intercollegiate football than the one we have with Michigan and Ohio State.

NONE!

There are some other great ones around the country. Every one of them is good for the sport and good for their schools.

But the Michigan/Ohio State rivalry is special. You can line up all the others and they still wind up as bridesmaids.

It doesn't matter what part of the country you talk about. This one is the best.

These two teams have played each other every year since 1918. And with the exception of 1942, it's been the last regular game of the season since 1935.

No other game annually has as much riding on it.

There's the conference championship. There's normally a Rose Bowl bid involved. And in some way, the national rankings always get a shake-up after this game.

On top of it all, it seems like the students at these two schools simply don't like each other.

When we coached against each other, the media made a big thing out of the "Woody/Bo Wars." I suppose all the hype was good for the game. But no one needs any extra motivation for this one. Players on both sides of the field don't worry about who's coaching on the other sideline.

But I have to admit...those battles were fun.

We were right here in Ann Arbor for the first one. Woody had his team on the field for practice when I was taking mine down the tunnel. I looked out and

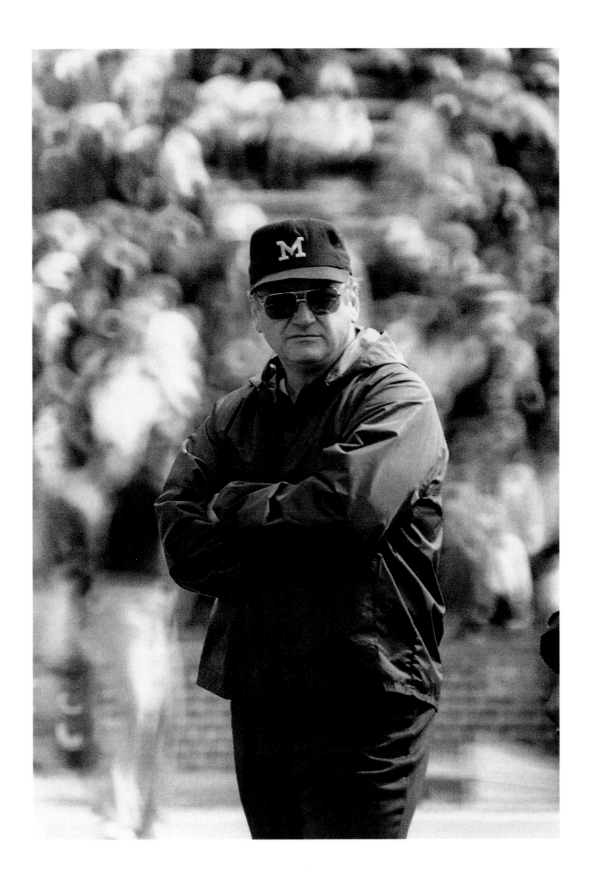

"Never go on that field down there without adequate protection."

saw Ohio State warming up on our side of the field.

I knew it was Woody. He already had coached a lot of games here. He knew where he was supposed to be. He was testing me. Now he's got my players watching to see what I would do.

I walked straight to him. Very calm. Very deliberate.

"Woody...you're warming up on the wrong side of the field," I said.

"You should be down at the other end."

He looked back. Very calm. Very deliberate.

"O.K.," he said. "We'll go down to that end. Come on men. Let's go."

My guys liked that. They knew this is our house and we set the rules.

That's the way he was, though. He'd always play little psychological games.

What a lot of people don't know is that Woody and I rarely talked to each other. We both respected each other. I admired him very much. But there was no cause for a lot of talking.

When all of the coaches got together at the Big Ten meetings in July we'd talk. That was it. In those 10 years we coached against each other, I never dialed the phone to call him and he never dialed the phone to talk to me.

That's just the way it was.

Before the games when we played, he'd tell one of my assistants, "You tell Coach Schembechler I'm ready to meet him at the 50."

My assistant would tell me and I'd go over to shake his hand. NEVER did I go over to his side of the 50. And NEVER did he step over to my side.

"Hi, Woody, how're you doing?" I'd ask him. "How's Anne?"

He'd say the same thing to me. That was it till the next year.

I loved the guy. I played for him. I coached for him. But that's just the way we always handled the situation.

I loved those games. We always knew what they were going to do and they knew what we were going to do. We both had each other's moves down cold.

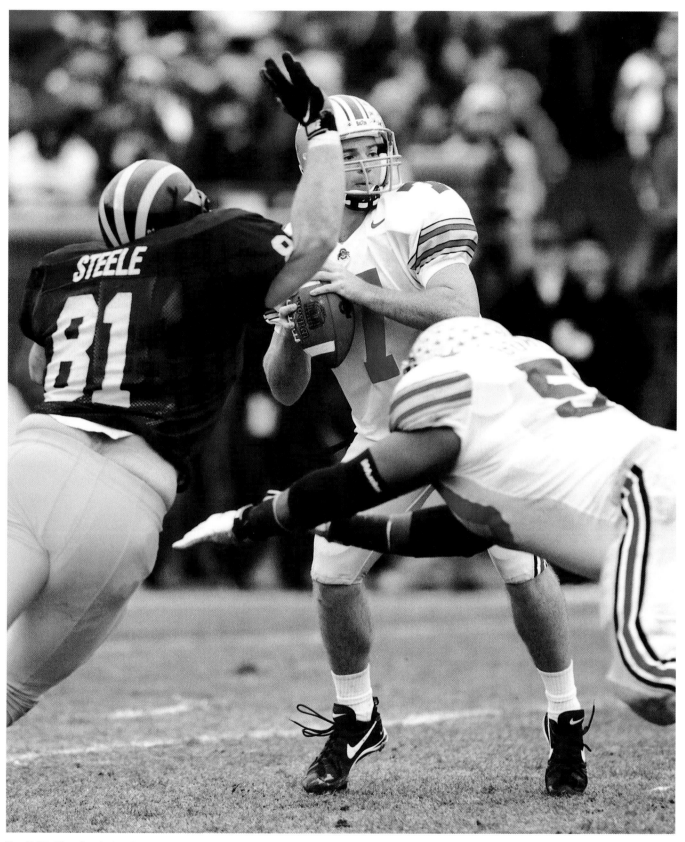

"In 1997, Glen Steele let that Buckeye quarterback know what this game is all about. If it looks rough, you should hear how it sounds down there."

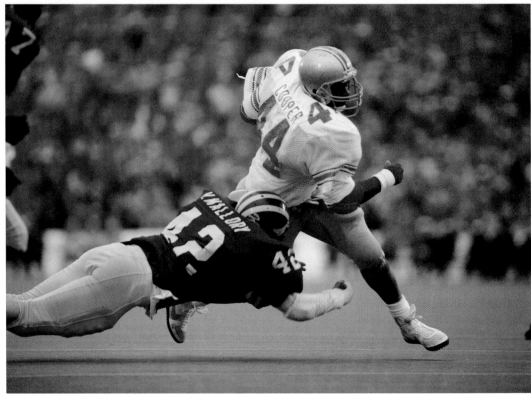

Captain Mike Mallory
was the first of three
of Coach Bill Mallory's
sons to play for
Michigan.

One thing everybody knew for sure was there was going to be some good old-fashioned, up close, hard-hitting football. I mean HARD-HITTING. It was punishing. It was real football.

When those two teams walked off that field after each one of those games, win or lose, both squads knew they had been in a football game.

That's what really made those games special. It still does. Those games are played with more intensity and more guts than anything you could make up for a Hollywood movie.

We did something in practice just for that game all year long. We made little adjustments that we saved just for them. They did the same thing for us.

It always got down to outblocking and outtackling the other guy and not making any mistakes. That's still the way it is today.

Woody and I tangled 10 times. Michigan finished on top, 5-4-1. That's pretty good against a school with the tradition of Ohio State. It shows just how tough this rivalry always has been. I'm proud of that.

After Woody retired, he called me one day during the season.

"Bo, this is Woody," he said. "I've got to give a speech up there."

"Good," I said. "Come out to practice."

When he arrived, I called my men together.

"Men, I want you to meet our old nemesis," I said. "This is the great Woody Hayes."

He talked to my men. It was a great scene.

This rivalry will outlive all of us. In college football, there is none better.

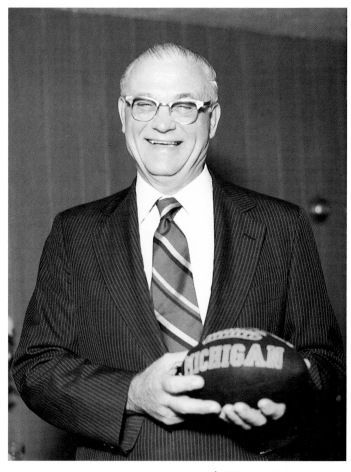

"You can bet your bottom dollar this was after he retired."

"BO, YOU'LL NEVER WIN A BIGGER GAME."

— Woody

In the middle of the Vietnam War...nation-wide civil unrest...various student protests...and a generally changing American society, Bo arrived at Michigan to change the face of Wolverine Football.

He didn't exactly tiptoe up U.S. 23 from Ohio. He more or less bulldozed through anything that stood in his way.

"Bo arrived in Ann Arbor the same way General Patton arrived in Europe," Dan

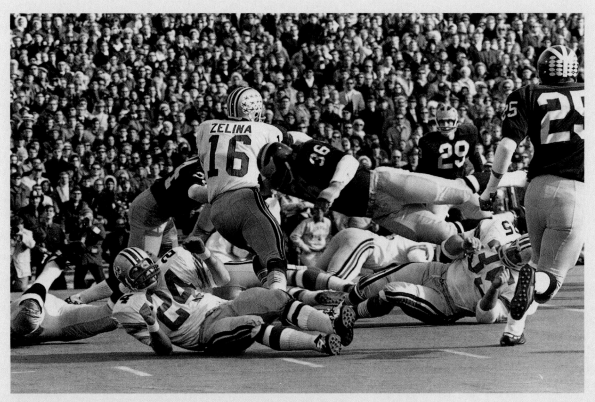

"My guys were simply not impressed by the Ohio State ranking."

Dierdorf said. "He's not exactly an inconspicuous person."

His arrival signaled the start of the modern era of Michigan Football.

"There's no question in my mind," Dierdorf said. "That 1969 season, and particularly the victory over Ohio State, took a program that had been O.K. since the late 1940s and vaulted it into something exceptional which hasn't stopped to this day."

Bo's program was simple. It was built on discipline, dedication, sweat, and blood. During spring practice of 1969, a lot of returning players did not survive the blitz.

"You have to recognize the climate of those times," said Jim Brandstatter, who is proud he stuck it out. "It was a very political era and the University was sort of the Berkeley of the Midwest."

Bo established a program of commitment

"Look at that scoreboard!"

that many felt more resembled Marine Corps training than a football camp.

"We took pride in the fact that there might have been a Marine brigade somewhere in the

"One of those special moments that will always live in my heart."

world better than us, but no one was in better shape," said Fritz Seyferth.

"There's a challenge and a testing of the mettle that we all have to go through in our lives. He tested ours. I promise you those who stayed acquired a whole different opinion of themselves and others and what can be accomplished with a commitment."

Many were unable to make that commitment. Spring practice started with about 125 players. By week's end, it had dwindled to about 85.

Even some who stayed at times questioned Bo's relentless drive.

"I was one of them," Dierdorf said. "But I was 19-years-old and what the heck did I know? Obviously, Bo was right and I was wrong."

Before practice began, Bo and his staff made their own commitment. Bo had that now-famous "Those Who Stay Will Be

Champions" sign hung in the locker room.

"During the week, one of the guys who quit took a Magic Marker and wrote under it, 'those who don't will be doctors and lawyers and other important people,'" Brandstatter said.

"But Bo made us all better men. There was never a time when we were physically or mentally stronger. I'll always be grateful for the experience."

In spite of an army of skeptics, Bo never doubted his program would work.

"According to the people who were here when I came, there was no way I could be successful," Bo said. "They said these methods would not work at Michigan. The University is a very liberal campus and kids simply would not accept that kind of discipline.

"They found out that if you present something that is good...if you are honest...and everyone wants to be successful...and this is

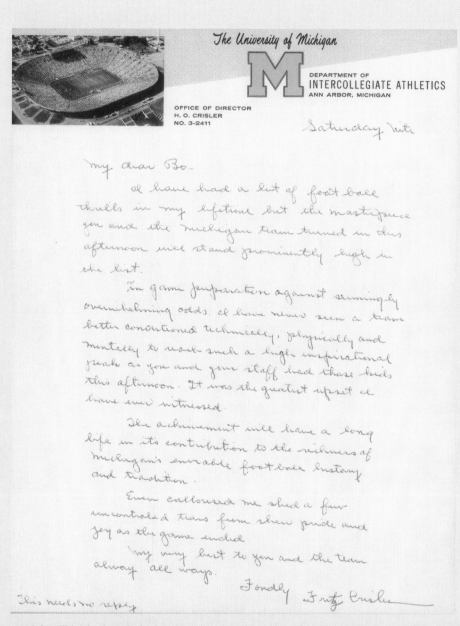

The University of Michigan

M DEPARTMENT OF
INTERCOLLEGIATE ATHLETICS
ANN ARBOR, MICHIGAN

OFFICE OF DIRECTOR
H. O. CRISLER
NO. 3-2411

"Fritz Crisler was lying ill in the hospital when he wrote me this letter after the 1969 win over Ohio State. When I read it I cried. It hangs on my wall at home."

the best way to achieve it...then they will accept it. They actually crave discipline if it's for the right reasons."

And so the modern era of Michigan Football was born.

"From the day Bo was carried off the field after we beat Ohio State in 1969, things have never been quite the same at the stadium or wherever Michigan goes," Dierdorf said. "We had beaten what many people considered to be the best college team ever assembled. We were perceived differently. And that's still true today."

Those who stay do, in fact, become champions.

GET IT RIGHT

Jim Brandstatter now laughs affectionately over the beginning of his lifelong friendship with Bo Schembechler.

At Tuesday's practice after Michigan suffered a blocked punt in a game the previous Saturday, the demonstration team blocked one on the varsity. Bo already had promised the demo team that anyone who blocked a punt would get a milk shake.

That wasn't quite what Brandstatter received.

"As soon as it happened, Bo came charging 40 yards down the field screaming," Brandstatter now recalls with a smile. "He was screaming: 'Brandstatter, you leave the field. You're the worst tackle in the history of intercollegiate football.'"

Brandstatter was stunned. He was moved to tears, thinking his Michigan football career was over in just his sophomore year. Actually, the defender had run over the player lined up next to him. One of the assistant coaches talked to Bo and told Brandstatter to stay.

On Friday, Bo approached Brandstatter.

"You don't think that was your fault, do you?" Bo asked.

"Coach, I know it wasn't my fault," Brandstatter answered.

"Well...you moved your feet too far apart anyway," Bo responded.

Now both teacher and student laugh about the incident. Both treasure their friendship of almost 30 years.

It wasn't until after he completed his Michigan football career in 1971 that Brandstatter fully appreciated Bo's design of developing character in young men.

"When you were a sophomore, all he tried to do was to push you," Brandstatter said. "He wanted you to become the best disciplined athlete and person you could possibly be. It was rough, but that's the only way he knew how to do it. And it worked.

"When you were a junior, you sort of understood what he was doing. By the time you became a senior, you realized your role of leadership. You then became a conduit to continue the tradition of Michigan Football. It's after you graduate, though, when you totally appreciate what Bo and Michigan Football has meant to your life. I could never thank either one of

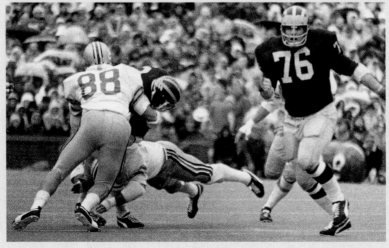

"Look at Jimmy's form. He's got a great career in broadcasting ahead of him."

them enough for what they mean to me."

Brandstatter played offensive tackle for the Wolverines from 1969-1971. Today he is a popular Detroit area radio and television football analyst for both the University of Michigan and the Detroit Lions.

He proudly states that his years at Michigan were "absolutely the best time of my life."

"It's hard to express, but the Michigan Football tradition is different than at other schools," he said.

"Uniforms change, year in and year out. Not at Michigan. Look at pictures of Tom Harmon and he's wearing that winged helmet. So is Ron Kramer. His No. 87 is retired. When he visits the program, those kids realize the importance of the past on the present and their responsibility to it.

"It's sort of like the attitude the Marines have for their uniform. They show tremendous respect for that uniform. It's the same at Michigan. When a young man puts on that maize and blue and that winged helmet, he's well aware of all the great ones who have gone before him. He knows he must perform to an expected level of excellence."

Brandstatter's admiration for Bo mirrors his respect for the Michigan Football tradition.

"He's honest," he said. "He's straightforward. He doesn't come in the side door. He's got the highest ethical standards and he's not afraid to let you know what they are.

"Most important is that he genuinely cares for people. He wants all young men who attend the University of Michigan to become the best football players they can possibly be. But he wants them to do it the right way. He wants them to do it with character."

Brandstatter marvels at Bo's unassuming humility.

"He truly is a legend," Brandstatter said. "But he just wants to be one of the guys. He never thinks what he accomplished is any great thing. He's a coach and he feels teaching and coaching is an admirable profession. That humility is not fake. He truly is the greatest living symbol of what the University of Michigan Football tradition is all about."

STILL AN "M" MAN

During the football off-seasons when he attended Michigan, Dan Dierdorf used to sit alone in the stadium.

"I love the place," he said. "When I was a freshman we couldn't play varsity. So I'd go over to the stadium and dream about how it would feel to come charging out of that tunnel for a game."

Over the next three seasons, he certainly got his chance. From 1968 through 1970, Dierdorf was one of the most feared offensive tackles in the country.

He was a consensus All-American in 1970. He later starred for the St. Louis Cardinals and was a 1996 inductee into the National Football League Hall of Fame. He is a long-time member of ABC television's Monday Night Football broadcast team.

"There's no way to describe just how big that stadium is when you come out of that

"He was the best offensive lineman I ever had."

tunnel," he said. "In the tunnel, you can't see anything. When you come out, it's like a snapshot. One minute you're in darkness and the next minute you're in the middle of the whole deal.

"It can take your breath away. You wouldn't want to put an EKG on the players in that tunnel. I'm sure there are a few skipped heartbeats. The resting pulse is probably 150. It's stressful, but it's tremendous."

Even after his Hall of Fame professional career and notoriety from being part of Monday Night Football, Dierdorf holds his college days at Michigan as one of the most precious parts of his life.

"There are so many images and friendships," he said. "Every time I see them, mentally I revert to being nineteen and twenty years old. I even think the way I did then. I'm assuming that will last till the day I die."

The tradition of Michigan Football still lives within Dierdorf.

"You can't be in Ann Arbor and participate in the football program without being aware of, and also honor bound to its tradition," he said. "It might sound hokey, but that tradition really is passed from class to class. It's a fiber that connects all of us.

"The thing that really impresses me is not only the length of its success, but also that it is a clean, above board and honorable program. All of us who have participated in the Michigan program realize there's a lot more to it than simply the wins in the record book."

Dierdorf was recruited to Michigan by Bump Elliott. He played his last two years under Bo Schembechler.

"I had the rare opportunity to be coached by one of the most remarkable personalities I've ever been around," Dierdorf said. "All of us who played for Bo were completely dominated by his will and personality. Most people are never in direct contact with someone who has that type of overwhelming personality.

"It's affected all of us. How often does it happen that you are in the circle of someone who is larger than life? It takes an exceptional man to drive 90 people as straight and as narrow as he drove us just on the strength of his will and sheer presence. We won because we were afraid to lose."

Dierdorf confirms that Bo always had a sense of humor as keen as his desire to win.

"That was one of his best qualities," Dierdorf said. "As demanding as he was, he could make the entire team laugh instantly. There were times we would just burst out laughing at something he said or did.

"One minute he'd be growling. And in the next breath he might say the guy who makes a great play will get a milk shake. We were always guessing at what was coming. That was his strong suit. I've never met anyone like him and I mean that in a most complimentary way. I'd do anything for the man."

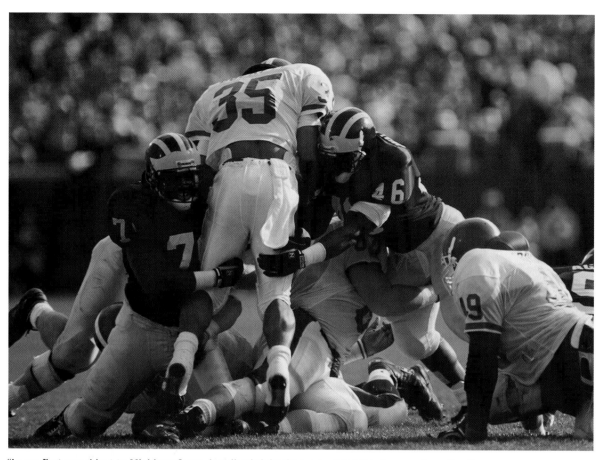

"In my first year I lost to Michigan State. I realized right then, I can't let this happen too often."

"That's Stan Edwards leaving white shirted Spartans behind."

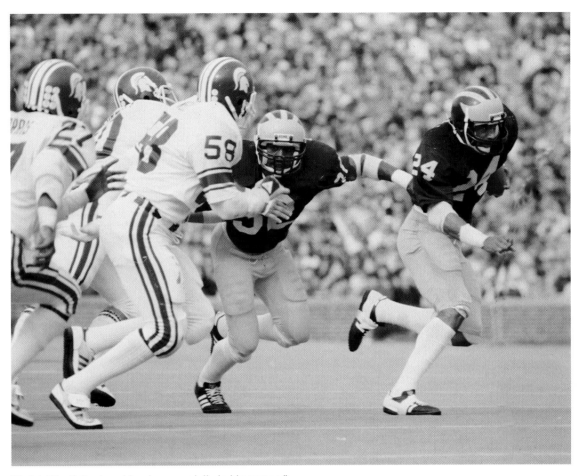

"Butch Woolfolk played hard — especially in big games."

"Coach Yost put on a Spartan blanket, but I bet he didn't wear it during the game."

"Sometimes the students get a little excited after big games."

"No, no Notre Dame."

"Notre Dame is, by far, the most intense non-conference rivalry."

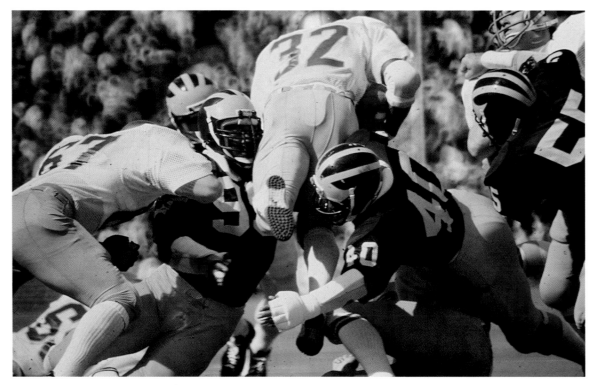

"Not against Michigan, you don't."

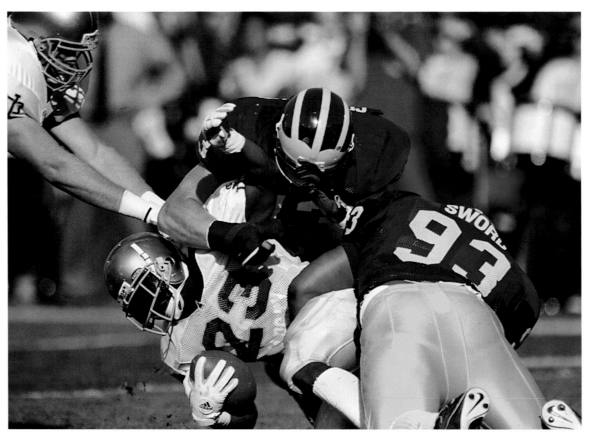

"A beautiful sight — a gold helmet down and that magnificent striped one on top."

"These guys haven't had much to cheer about the last several years."

"Yes, we have some of those too."

"The Paul Bunyan Trophy was initiated by Governor G. Mennen Williams in 1953 and goes to the winner of the Michigan-Michigan State game. It looks nice in Ann Arbor."

THE REAL THING

The real Little Brown Jug is locked in a wooden box and carefully stored in the equipment room in Schembechler Hall.

Equipment Manager Jon Falk is responsible for its security. He brings it out on the day of the Michigan-Minnesota game and carries it to the field where one of his assistants guards it on the sidelines.

The winner of the game keeps the treasured jug until the two teams meet the following year. For more than the last half century, the Little Brown Jug has found a home in Ann Arbor. Going into the 1998 season, Michigan has beaten Minnesota in 44 of its last 55 meetings, including 28 of the last 30 and 11 in a row.

The battle for the Little Brown Jug literally is the granddaddy of all intercollegiate football trophy games. There are 57 such games played annually around the country. All owe their creation to this traditional rivalry.

It started back in 1903 in Minnesota. Michigan Coach Fielding Yost doubted that his rival would supply pure water to the Michigan bench. He ordered one of his staff to purchase a jug to avoid any problem.

After Minnesota scored late for a 6-6 tie, pandemonium broke out in the stands. The game was called with time left on the clock. In their haste to leave, Michigan left the jug on the field. It was discovered by Minnesota equipment manager Oscar Munson who gave it to his athletic director. On the jug, the Gophers painted: "Michigan Jug – Captured by Oscar, October 31, 1903," and the score "Minnesota 6, Michigan 6."

When Yost sent a letter requesting the jug's return, the Minnesota athletic director wrote back, "If you want it, you'll have to come up and win it."

And over the years, Michigan certainly has.

The two teams did not meet again until 1909 when Michigan won, 15-6.

The jug disappeared from Michigan's trophy case in 1930 and was missing until 1934. Before the actual jug was found behind a clump of bushes by a gas station attendant in Ann Arbor, a replica stood in the trophy case. The authenticity of the original was confirmed by a flaw that could not have been duplicated.

Now the jug has truly found a home. And it truly is the real thing.

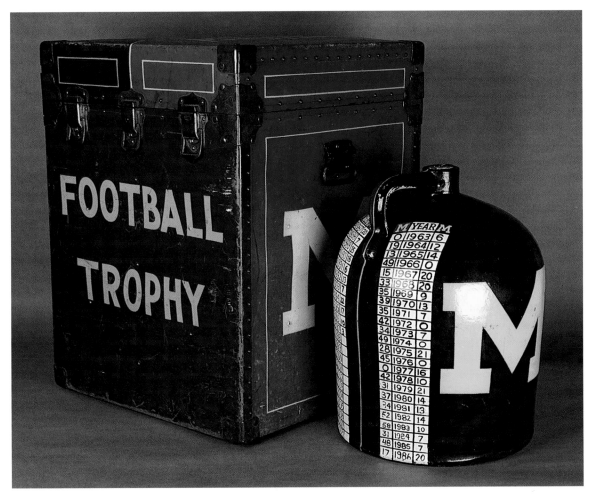

"I never realized how important the Little Brown Jug was until we lost it."

ROSES IN THE SNOW

It snowed the day after Thanksgiving in 1950. On the next day in Columbus, a blizzard struck so fiercely that it was almost impossible to see the field.

Nature nudged its way into creating a chunk of college football folklore with the "Snow Bowl" in Columbus.

There were 50,503 fans caked in icicles as the Wolverines and Buckeyes battled in conditions better suited for polar bears. Nearly a half-century later, the game still is relived in wonder, even by those who were born long after the historical event.

"We bussed to Toledo before taking the train to Columbus," said Michigan fullback Don Dufek. "When we got there, the train parked on a rail. We looked out the windows and saw all these people slipping and sliding and falling down."

Dufek still smiles when recalling the scene.

"All the coaches walked down the aisle and yelled 'pull your shades down,'" he said. "I guess they didn't want us to see how bad the conditions were."

But the game was played. And it still sparkles brightly in the treasure chest of college football memories.

Despite heroic efforts to keep the field clean by sweeping between plays, snow and ice made it impossible for either team to move the ball. Not only couldn't they move it, they had trouble merely seeing the yard lines.

The teams combined on a staggering 45 punts. Michigan could not make a first down. Ohio State eked out two.

But Michigan persisted. After falling behind by a field goal that, at the time, must have looked as secure as Fort Knox, Michigan rallied to block two punts – one for a safety and another for a touchdown.

"Two guys who really deserve a lot of credit were Chuck Ortmann and Carl Kreager," Dufek said. "Ortmann did a great job of punting all day. Kreager was the center. Despite the conditions, he did not make one bad snap."

And the magic went beyond Columbus. While Michigan doggedly defeated both Ohio State and Mother Nature, in Evanston, Northwestern upset Illinois to vault the Wolverines into the Rose Bowl.

Pitted against undefeated California, Michigan rallied with a pair of fourth quarter touchdowns to upset the 4th-ranked Golden Bears, 14-6. It was Dufek who scored both Michigan touchdowns and was named the game's Most Valuable Player.

"It sounds poetic," he said, "but I guess there really were roses in that snow at Columbus."

And forever that miserable snow and ice and beautiful roses will remain a piece of Michigan tradition.

MOMSEN—M.

"That's Tony Momsen recovering a fumble for the only touchdown in the 1950 'Snow Bowl'. Games like that separate the men from the boys."

OHIO STATE COACHING STAFF

Front row, left to right: Gene Fekete, junior varsity coach; Bo Schembechler, assistant junior varsity coach; Bill Arnsparger, tackle coach; Bill Hess, guard coach. Back row: Doyt Perry, backfield coach; Harry Strobel, defensive line coach; W. W. (Woody) Hayes, head coach; Esco Sarkkinen, end coach; Ernie Godfrey, assistant line coach.

"That was an outstanding coaching staff at Ohio State. Look how young Woody (middle, standing) looks. And how about that guy Schembechler (kneeling, second from left)?"

THE OHIO STATE UNIVERSITY
AREA OF STUDENT RELATIONS
INTERCOLLEGIATE ATHLETICS
ST. JOHN ARENA
410 WEST WOODRUFF
COLUMBUS, OHIO 43210

Office of Director

AREA CODE 614
TELEPHONE: 293-2341

Dear Bo,

[handwritten letter]

Woody and I didn't talk often. However, following my heart attack on the eve of the 1970 Rose Bowl game, Woody sent a letter of encouragement.

He asked, "If you were going to have a sick spell why didn't you have it at our game, for your team didn't look the same without you? On television it appeared that they stuck in there real well but they lacked the coordination that they had against us."

He closed saying, "I'll see you next November 21st."

Your old coach,
Woody

CAPTURED IN TIME

Let me tell you something. The day this stops being a meaningful experience for the guys who play is the day we ought to throw the whole damn thing out.

— Bo Schembechler

ometimes it takes just one game. Sometimes it takes a whole season.

There's a point, though, in every great program where something jumps up and tells everybody in the United States of America — hey, we've got something special here.

For me, it was our 1969 victory over Ohio State. That one game made my program. Now we move along to the present and we've got the 1997 team.

In case somebody has been living under a rock and hasn't noticed, Lloyd Carr and his players have made one helluva statement.

Michigan Football is back where it's supposed to be — right on TOP!

There's no other sport like college football where games played 20, 30, or even 50 years ago are just as alive today as they were back then.

We remember key plays. We know what the weather was like. We're able to throw ourselves back in time and feel all of the things that were going on around us.

That's the beauty of college football. As long as there are people around who were there when the game was played, the memories live forever. At a place like Michigan with its long tradition, even some of those games that are 60 and 70 years old keep on getting replayed like one of those old classic movies.

In my career, I was fortunate to have been part of some mighty big ones. Rose Bowls...Ohio State games...Michigan State games.

If I had to pick one, though, none was more important than that 24-12 whipping we put on Ohio State in my first season in 1969.

"Anthony Thomas doesn't only carry the ball, he carries a legacy."

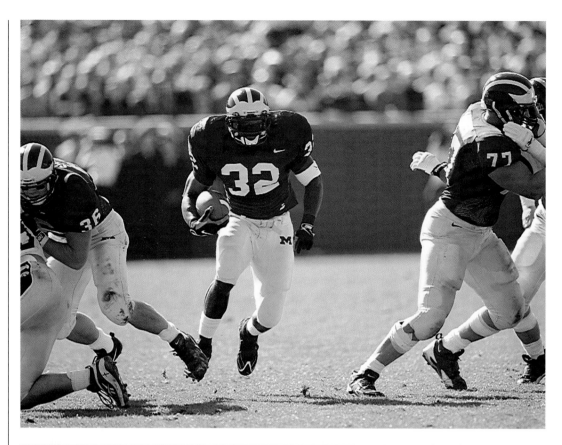

"Every catch seems to be just a little bit better against Ohio State. Just ask Mercury Hayes."

"No one shredded the Ohio State defense like Tshimanga Biakabutuka did with 313 yards in 1995."

That one game sent a message to the whole country. From that day forward, Michigan was back where it was supposed to be.

We were going to be a force to be reckoned with from here on out!

After Woody Hayes retired, I was invited to speak at a banquet in his honor. Security was tight. The only people allowed into the hall were his former players and any assistant who ever coached for him.

I was still coaching at Michigan and I was selected to speak on behalf of all the former assistants.

Some people may have had a little trouble understanding Woody. But I loved the man. He was honest. He was totally dedicated to his beliefs and his team. He was a man of high integrity. And he knew more about football than most coaches in the country put together.

I got up and spoke my piece. When I was finished, Woody walked up to the podium. Before he started, he spotted Dick Brubaker — one of his old players — all the way in the back of the room smoking a cigarette.

"Brubaker," he barked. "Put the damn cigarette out before I start. Now I'm not going to talk if anybody out there is smoking."

Every cigar and cigarette in the place went out. It didn't matter how long ago any of those guys had played for him. No former players were going to smoke when the old coach was speaking.

"That's going the little extra against Ohio State."

"We had so many great teams here," Woody began. "We had national championships. We have so much to be proud of. But that 1969 squad was probably the most talented football team I ever had. It was a marvelous team."

He proceeded to rattle off a list of names like Rex Kern, Jim Otis, John Brockington, Jack Tatum, and a whole lot more. Then he stopped. He looked down at the end of the table where I was sitting.

"Damn you, Bo," he growled. "You will never win a bigger game than that one!"

Every person in the place roared. We all knew he was right. That one game was the catalyst for everything that came after it at Michigan.

Almost every football expert in every part of the United States of America agreed that the 1969 Ohio State squad was the greatest college team ever assembled.

They were undefeated and national champions in 1968. They were 8-0 and rated No. 1 when they came into Ann Arbor that day. Nobody but my players, my coaches, me, and God thought we even had a chance to stay within two touchdowns of those guys.

But we did it. We did it because we had made a commitment way back around Christmas when I got to Ann Arbor that we were going to beat those guys and put Michigan back where it belongs.

The previous year in Columbus, Woody stuck a knife into Michigan. That wound did not heal till 12 months later when we knocked them off their No. 1 perch. Late in that 1968 game, he went for a two-point conversion after a touchdown to make the score 50-14.

Well, no one at Michigan ever forgot that. I made damn sure none of my players forgot.

CAPTURED IN TIME

Every day starting in spring practice, we did something special to prepare for that game.

The Saturday before that game we went up to Iowa and crushed them, 51-6. And Iowa had a pretty decent team.

After that game before the team even went into the locker room, all the guys gathered in this meeting room. They kept shouting: "Beat Ohio...Beat Ohio...Beat Ohio." They were pounding on each other's shoulders. They were slapping helmets. I mean, man, they were physical.

One of my coaches said, "Bo, they're going to get too high."

I said, "Leave them alone. We will NEVER be too high for this game. Let 'em go."

That whole week before the Ohio State game, I had every one of my demonstration team players wear No. 50 for practice.

"Brian Griese stepped up and became a true 'Michigan Man' in 1997.

It was a wild week. First it snowed. Then we got sleet. The field was unplayable so I had all the freshmen and other guys out there with brooms and shovels so we could practice. The practices were good and crisp, but the weather was terrible.

It was frigid that Friday night before the game. The furnace blew out in the hotel where we were staying. At 2 o'clock in the morning, I got up and rounded up a bunch of blankets. We went around to all the players' rooms and gave them extra blankets.

Everything that could go wrong that week did go wrong. Except for one thing. None of my boys forgot what had happened the previous year.

We took a 24-12 lead into halftime and that same frenzy happened all over again. Jim

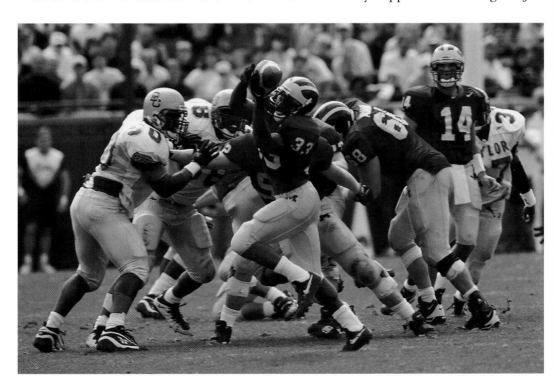

187

Young was one of my coaches. He was very smart but not a very demonstrative sort of person.

He jumped up and yelled: "They will NOT score in the second half! THEY WILL NOT SCORE!"

And, by God, they didn't.

We were ranked 12th going into that game and pulled off one of the biggest upsets in history. Nobody was supposed to beat Ohio State. Not even the great Green Bay Packers.

Well, we did. And Michigan wasn't a 'Nobody' any more.

By the time I got home that night, I was getting phone calls from the media all over the country. It exploded. From that day forward, everybody knew Michigan was back. And you better get ready to deal with us.

Now during the last few seasons, Michigan never failed to win at least eight games. But four losses a year simply doesn't get it, according to Michigan standards.

Lloyd Carr was placed into an awfully awkward position. He took over the team under very difficult circumstances. Even when he was put in charge before the 1995 season, he was termed the "interim coach."

That's tough at any school. At Michigan, it's working with handcuffs.

When you're an interim, how do you go about recruiting the right kids to perform on a national level? How do you go about putting together the right coaching staff?

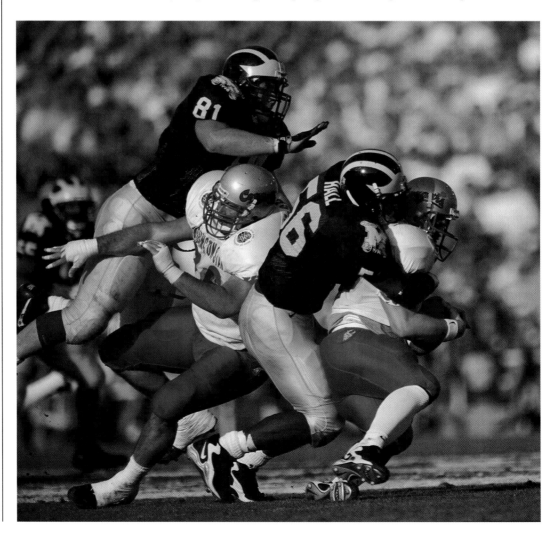

Well, he did it. He did it quietly. He did it meticulously. And he did it with integrity.

Lloyd Carr went about putting all the pieces together and created his own program that perfectly reflects the Michigan tradition.

Lloyd recruited extremely well. The 1997 team belonged to him. He's one of the best recruiters I've ever seen. That's because he's honest...he cares about the kids who come here...and he's concerned that the kids who do commit to Michigan are the kind of kids who appreciate what the Michigan tradition is all about.

The kids he has today could have played at Michigan in any era. There isn't one of them who cares more about himself than he does about the TEAM.

Success in football is not the result of the individual. It's the combined efforts of the whole TEAM.

That's pretty much true of almost every successful operation in life. And it's damn sure true of how that 1997 team performed from the first day it stepped foot on the field in spring practice!

That squad had its share of very talented individuals. Not one of them, though, was bigger than the whole team. And that's the way they played for four quarters in each one of their 12 games.

Right from the start, there wasn't a Michigan fan on the planet that couldn't sense something special was happening.

Colorado was supposed to be a national power. When Michigan dominated every single part of that game to open the season, everyone could feel — MICH-igan is back!

No coach, no player, not anyone associated with the team took one game for granted. No one let up for even one play. This was a team that was committed to excellence. This was a team that everyone could love.

It's fun to cheer for an individual to have a great season. But the fun is so much sweeter when that love can be shared with the whole team.

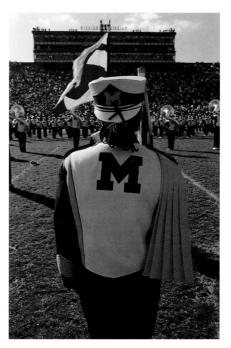

"The backwards hat symbolizes another Michigan victory. The band members are used to that."

189

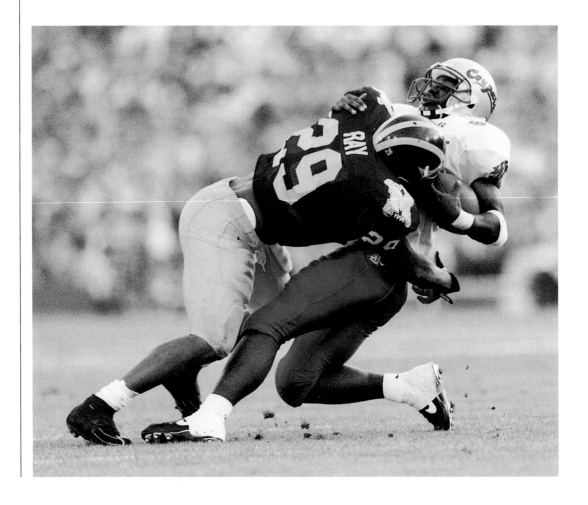

That team didn't wake up one day and just happen. It was three years in the making. And that one season certainly made a statement.

It states that Michigan is back. It states that this is Lloyd Carr's program. It states that anyone who plays for this program is playing for Michigan and not for himself. And it states that this program is going to be around for a long time to come!

Years from now people will still be talking about how the 1997 Michigan team completely dominated Colorado in the first game of the season. They'll talk about how they traveled to Michigan State and Penn State and absolutely overwhelmed two very fine football teams. They'll talk about beating Ohio State to go to the Rose Bowl. And they'll talk about beating Washington State in Pasadena to capture the National Championship.

Each one of those games actually gets bigger as the years roll along. Each one of those touchdowns by the offense and each one of those dramatic stops by the defense will get bigger and bigger.

I don't think any Michigan fan will truly appreciate just how much that 1997 team means to Michigan tradition until a few years from now.

This is something very special here. This is pure Michigan tradition.

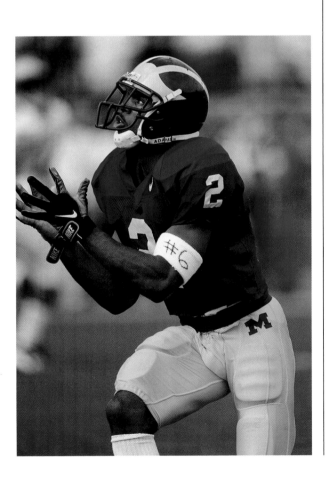

LAST BOWL BEFORE BO

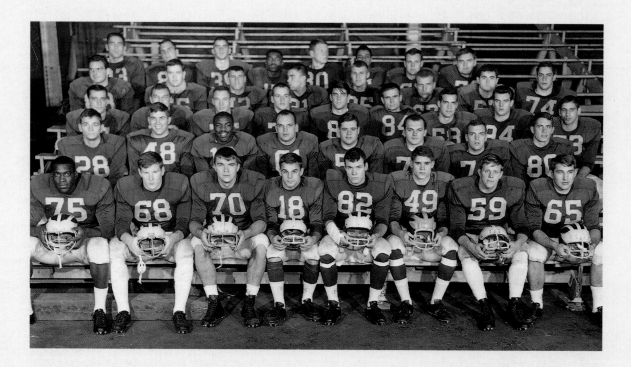

Until Bo turned Michigan into a perennial postseason participant, the Wolverines' lone bowl appearance between 1951 and 1970 came in the 1965 Rose Bowl.

Michigan made the most of that opportunity by squashing Oregon State, 34-7.

For those young men growing up during the turbulent political decade of the '60s, the experience left lifetime memories. Jim Conley captained that team. And he's proud of it for more than just its on-field success.

"In those days, only 44 players were allowed to dress for the Rose Bowl," said Conley. "All but two graduated from Michigan."

That's an incredibly high percentage, but that also was an incredibly gifted team. Except for a 21-20 upset to unranked Purdue in the season's fourth game, Michigan was flawless. The Wolverines outscored their opponents, 235-83. They finished 9-1 and ranked 4th nationally.

Conley carries many fond memories from his Michigan career. None, however, remain as warm as Michigan's 10-0 shutout at Ohio State in the game before that Rose Bowl.

"It was so cold," Conley said. "But we were so excited. I actually felt like I was floating in the air above the field watching everything that was going on down there."

Conley must have enjoyed what he saw because he turned in a spectacular performance. He played end on both sides of the ball and wound up with 12 tackles and 13 assists. Conley was a friend of Bo Rein who played on that Ohio State team.

"He said that Woody Hayes told his guys after the game, 'How could you let that skinny S.O.B. Conley beat you?'" Conley laughed.

Although always competitive, the Michigan teams during that period were not as dominant as after Bo's arrival. Conley played under Bump Elliott, who had been an outstanding player and became a very solid coach. Through the years, Conley has gotten to know Bo well.

"Bo did more for college football than any other one man," Conley said.

"They used to take just 44 players to the Rose Bowl. Bo argued that if they can take 250 members from the band and 300 faculty members then he should be able to take his whole squad. He said he wouldn't go if he couldn't. Bo also was largely responsible for getting the Big Ten to allow its members to play in more games than just the Rose Bowl."

Even more significant to Conley is the manner in which Bo conducted the program.

"Everything was by the book," Conley said. "There was never anything done under the table. Everything was done up front and no individual was bigger than the team."

"Bo symbolizes the Michigan tradition. It's about the team. It's about winning and graduating. He could be a poster boy for what college athletics should be."

Those were some of the precise reasons why Conley chose Michigan over Penn State, Notre Dame, and Dartmouth after graduating from Springdale (PA) High School in 1961.

"There is no other place like the University of Michigan," he said. "You get to meet those who went before you. Guys like Ron Kramer. And you meet those who come afterward. It may sound corny but it really is a big family."

As a sophomore in 1962, Conley and his teammates had the privilege of listening to the legendary Fritz Crisler deliver a speech to them the Friday night before the Ohio State game.

"He was such a powerful speaker," Conley said. "It was moving. I thought some guys were going to cry."

Maybe the speech had some impact because Michigan took Ohio State to a scoreless tie at the half before the Buckeyes ground out a 28-0 victory.

"Imagine what we might have done if Mr. Crisler had spoken at breakfast," Conley cracked.

Nevertheless, it was then that the team made a promise to get back to the Rose Bowl soon. Two years later that promise was kept.

"When I sat in the stands as a freshman, I saw how much Michigan football means to so many people," Conley said. "There are a lot of good football programs around the country. There are a lot of good academic schools. But how many combine those two elements as well as Michigan? None."

Conley is a successful manufacturer's representative for the automobile industry in Dearborn. He still resides in Ann Arbor and remains as rabid a fan as he was a player. Occasionally he's asked to address the team.

That's an easy job for the old captain. That passion for Michigan is one that simply doesn't die.

ATTITUDE MEANS VICTORY

There is no more important job for the head coach than to create a winning attitude. His primary responsibility is to make sure that every member of the organization maintains the same positive attitude and desire to win. That applies to all the players, all the assistant coaches and all the people who work in the department.

Each coach has his own way of developing attitude. But it must be done before success is realized.

That's a 24-hour a day, seven-day a week job. The head coach must create that attitude and he better work on it on a daily basis.

It's very easy to see in a football player someone who is not performing up to expectations. The head coach must find out why that is happening and he must address the problem immediately!

I've always felt that when a problem exists in an individual player or with a team, you must attack that problem now. You do not take the problem home. You do not sleep on it. You attack. If you have attacked it incorrectly, you can always apologize. But if you let that problem sit, you can not have a good, tough, disciplined football program. That's impossible.

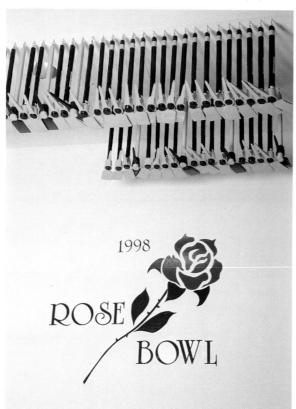

1998 ROSE BOWL

Without attitude, there is no victory!

You can not develop that attitude on game day. You can not do it simply in a pre-game meeting with a "win one for the Gipper" speech. That can help. But that alone won't get the job done. Attitude must be built at the beginning of the year. Then it must be maintained daily throughout the season.

Everyone saw what Lloyd Carr did with the 1997 team. That was the result of attitude. And it didn't just happen overnight.

As long as I coached and even today in retirement, the first thing I look for is when the team comes out of that tunnel. Right then I can tell if the team is ready to play that day. More than anything else, that is the responsibility of the head coach.

Attitude is a daily job. And how well you perform that job determines how well the team will finish.

"Coach Carr inspired his 1997 team that each play of each game must be executed one step at a time, just like climbing that impossible mountain. Each player received a pick that hung in the team meeting room thoughout the season. Once they made it to the top, each one received his pick symbolic of that long climb to the National Championship."

194

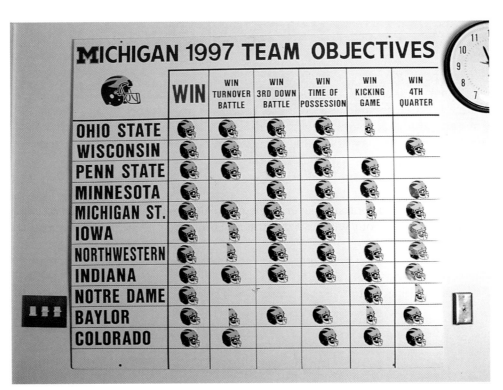

MICHIGAN 1997 TEAM OBJECTIVES						
	WIN	WIN TURNOVER BATTLE	WIN 3RD DOWN BATTLE	WIN TIME OF POSSESSION	WIN KICKING GAME	WIN 4TH QUARTER
OHIO STATE	●	●	●	●	●	
WISCONSIN	●	●	●	●		●
PENN STATE	●	●	●	●	●	
MINNESOTA	●	●	●	●		●
MICHIGAN ST.	●	●	●	●	●	●
IOWA	●	●	●	●		●
NORTHWESTERN	●	●	●	●	●	●
INDIANA	●	●	●	●	●	●
NOTRE DAME	●				●	●
BAYLOR	●	●	●	●	●	●
COLORADO	●	●		●	●	●

"Champions must set goals and then stick to them."

"We certainly know how to draw a crowd."

"The Cadets have arrived. And Michigan is going to march them right out."

THE TOUCHDOWN THAT NEVER WAS

"It was a fumble then...and it's still a fumble now."

That's the way Bo and most of the rest of a disbelieving national television audience saw the play on which Charles White scored a phantom touchdown in Southern California's 17-10 victory over Michigan in the 1979 Rose Bowl.

"It was so obvious," Bo still maintains today. "It wasn't even close. White was hit before he crossed the plane (of the goal line) and fumbled the ball on the three-yard line."

The controversial play occurred in the second quarter with USC leading, 7-3.

"If that call had been made properly, we had a chance to win," Bo said. "Stopping that drive and recovering the fumble put momentum on our side."

To this day, Bo understands perhaps why the line judge first made the call. But he still does not understand why the other officials did not overrule the decision.

"There might have been players on his (line judge) side of the field that hid his view," Bo said. "When White dived, the official assumed he had the ball. Well, the ball was back on the three-yard line where Jerry Meter recovered it."

The umpire, in fact, signaled first down for Michigan. But he was overruled by the official who first made the call.

"It was the worst call I'd ever seen," Bo said.

Long after the game, Bo commiserated with his coaches in his hotel room. The sports news was on television and White was being interviewed.

"The funny thing was when White was explaining he had scored a touchdown, the reporters had a record of Frank Sinatra's song 'It's Impossible' playing in the background," Bo said.

A few years later, Bo ran into White at a Heisman Trophy banquet.

"I walked up to him and said, 'White you fumbled that ball,'" Bo said. "He looked at me and smiled and said, 'ah...well,'"

It was the touchdown that never happened. As Bo says...it was a fumble then and is still a fumble now.

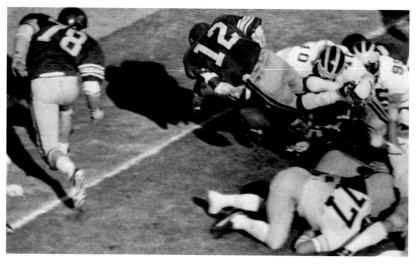

"That's the 1979 Rose Bowl and that's still a fumble by USC's Charles White!"

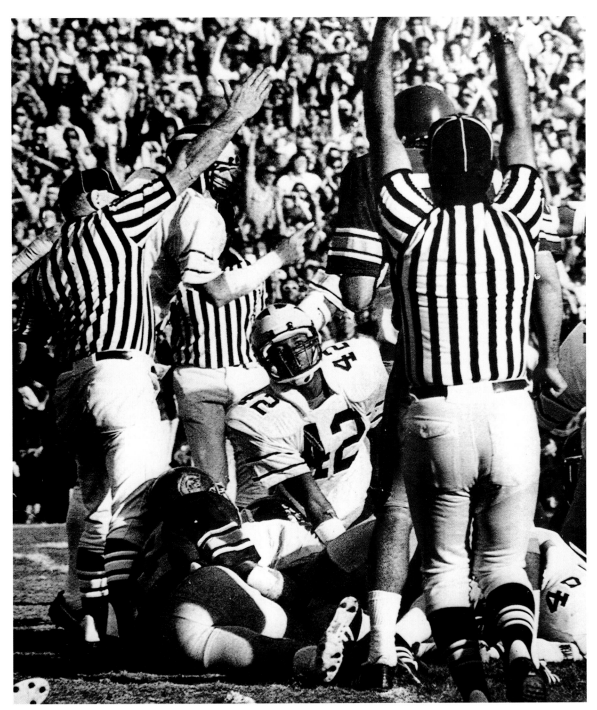

"At least one official got it right."

A TIME
FOR THANKS

Success in the future is based upon success of the past.

— Bo Schembechler

alking off the field after we beat Ohio State in 1989, I pretty much knew it would be my last trip through that tunnel.

I didn't give it much thought at the time. We had just beaten Ohio State, 28-18. Any game with that team is a killer for both sides. And we had to start preparing for the Rose Bowl.

But I sort of knew.

Looking back, it's easier to put things into perspective. And the bottom line is how amazingly powerful Michigan Football really is.

Fielding H. Yost once coached here. Then he was gone.

Fritz Crisler coached here. So did Bennie Oosterbaan and Bump Elliott.

All of them were marvelous. All of them made tremendous contributions. But no single man is responsible for the overall excellence of the Michigan tradition.

In academics or athletics, the true test of excellence is time. No other yardstick is a greater measure.

Success in the classroom or on the football field often is discovered by the good ones. The great ones, however, are able to do it year after year after year.

That's the mark of a champion. And for more than a century now, that's the standard which the University of Michigan has set.

That is the heart and soul of tradition. And it's as alive today as it was before Fielding H. Yost even came up with the idea to dig that big hole in the ground and build the most magnificent stadium in college football anywhere in the country.

203

It's been 30 years now since I was first given the privilege of becoming part of this great tradition. There were many great moments. There were a few I'd like to forget.

But I wouldn't trade one second for having had the opportunity to become at least one small part of the greatest university in the world.

We won championships. We won bowl games. Hopefully we created memories which every Michigan graduate and fan will cherish for a lifetime.

More importantly than all of that, we accomplished all those things by doing it the Michigan way. We did it with honesty and integrity.

Today, I get no bigger thrill than going out to that stadium on a fall Saturday afternoon. I sit up in the press box now. Before the game starts, I look around at all those people packed into those stands. I appreciate how much that football team means to all of them.

And when I watch those young men come charging out of that tunnel, I still get the same chills as I did when I ran out of there for all those years.

Each game is a battle because each game is for Michigan. I can feel all those goose bumps that the players and the coaches and the trainers and everyone on the field gets. And I know — win or lose — those young men are going to fight for MICH-i-gan. They won't leave that field till every drop of sweat is gone.

Coach Lloyd Carr appreciates the significance of the Michigan tradition. He honors it. He understands that success in the future is based on the success of the past. No one person is bigger than the University.

That's exactly why his football teams will continue to excel. They'll succeed under the same Michigan standards that were established long before he or I arrived in Ann Arbor. They'll succeed because of hard work...dedication...honesty...and integrity.

Somewhere down the road, Coach Carr will be gone. Another coach will receive the privilege of becoming part of the finest football program in the country.

The University of Michigan is about excellence. And it's filled with tra-DI-tion!

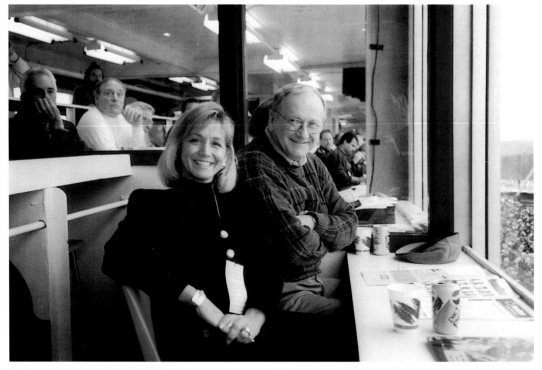

Cathy never saw me coach or she probably never would have married me.

PHOTO CREDITS

THE MILLIE SCHEMBECHLER
ADRENAL CANCER RESEARCH FUND

The Millie Schembechler Adrenal Cancer Research Fund was created in 1993 in honor of Bo's wife who had died the previous year. It was Bo's goal to establish the University of Michigan Hospital as the world's foremost research center for the disease.

Since 1993, Bo has staged a one-day charity golf tournament each summer to raise funds. With Bo serving as chairman and Howard Wikel as president of the Millie Schembechler Memorial Foundation, the organization has raised approximately $2.5 million of the $3.5 million goal it set for the year 2000.

At present, adrenal cancer has no cure. Through the efforts of the Foundation and the generosity of supporters from around the country, research continues toward discovery of a cure.

A portion of the sales of this book will be designated to the Foundation. For anyone wishing to contribute separately, please send out a check made out to the Millie Schembechler Adrenal Cancer Research Fund to the attention of the Fund at:

Schembechler Hall
1200 South State Street
Ann Arbor, MI 48109

The Foundation, the hospital, and all concerned thank you.